The Legend of Zelda: A Link to the Past

Unauthorized Game Secrets

NOW AVAILABLE

Alone in the Dark 3: The Official Strategy Guide
Caesar II: The Official Strategy Guide
Celtic Tales: Balor of the Evil Eye—The Official Strategy Guide
Cyberia: The Official Strategy Guide
Cyberia2: The Official Strategy Guide
Dark Seed II: The Official Strategy Guide
Descent: The Official Strategy Guide
Descent II: The Official Strategy Guide
DOOM Battlebook
DOOM II: The Official Strategy Guide
Dragon Lore: The Official Strategy Guide
Fleet Defender: The Official Strategy Guide
Front Page Sports Football Pro '95: The Official Playbook
Fury3: The Official Strategy Guide
Hell: A Cyberpunk Thriller—The Official Strategy Guide
Heretic: The Official Strategy Guide
King's Quest VII: The Unauthorized Strategy Guide
Lords of Midnight: The Official Strategy Guide
Marathon: The Official Strategy Guide
Master of Magic: The Official Strategy Guide
MechWarrior 2: The Official Strategy Guide
Microsoft Flight Simulator 5.1: The Official Strategy Guide
Shannara: The Official Strategy Guide
SimCity 2000: Power, Politics, and Planning
SimEarth: The Official Strategy Guide
SimFarm Almanac: The Official Guide to SimFarm
SimLife: The Official Strategy Guide
SimTower: The Official Strategy Guide
SubWar 2050: The Official Strategy Guide
Thunderscape: The Official Strategy Guide
Under a Killing Moon: The Official Strategy Guide
WarCraft: Orcs & Humans Official Secrets & Solutions
WarCraft II: Tides of Darkness—The Official Strategy Guide
Warlords II Deluxe: The Official Strategy Guide
Werewolf Vs. Commanche: The Official Strategy Guide
Wing Commander I, II, and III: The Ultimate Strategy Guide
X-COM UFO Defense: The Official Strategy Guide
X-Wing Collector's CD-ROM: The Official Strategy Guide

HOW TO ORDER

For information on quantity discounts contact the publisher: Prima Publishing, P.O. Box 1260BK, Rocklin, CA 95677-1260. On your letterhead include information concerning the intended use of the books and the number of books you wish to purchase.

The Legend of Zelda: A Link to the Past

Unauthorized Game Secrets

Zach Meston

PRIMA PUBLISHING
Rocklin, California
(916) 632-4400
www.primagames.com

Important:
Prima Publishing has made every effort to determine that the information contained in this book is accurate. However, the publisher makes no warranty, either expressed or implied, as to the accuracy, effectiveness, or completeness of the material in this book; nor does the publisher assume liability for damages, either incidental or consequential, that may result from using the information in this book. The publisher cannot provide information regarding game play, hints and strategies, or problems with hardware or software. Questions should be directed to the support numbers provided by the game and device manufacturers in their documentation. Some game tricks require precise timing and may require repeated attempts before the desired result is achieved.

ISBN: 1-55958-204-9
Printed in the United States of America

99 00 AA 28 27 26 25 24 23 22

Acknowledgments

Wow! I get a whole page of acknowledgments to myself! And it's about damn time, too. (Heh heh.)

- Thanks to Rusel DeMaria for finally giving me a book of my own. For a while there, I was considering changing my name to "Rusel DeMaria and Zach Meston." (Just kidding, Rusel.)
- Thanks to everyone at Prima for keeping me on track: Laurie Stewart, Roger Stewart, Debbie Parisi, Nancy Martinelli, and especially Kim Bartusch.
- Thanks to Mario DeLecce for his gameplaying efforts.
- Thanks to Andy Eddy and Chris Bieniek at *VideoGames & Computer Entertainment* for allowing me the pleasure of writing reviews for their great magazine.
- Thanks to Peggy Herrington and the mysterious Deb for all their help in navigating the occasionally baffling GEnie network. And for being my friends, too.
- Thanks to Danny Han for giving me a place to bash Sendai publications in his killer MS-DOS gaming fanzine, *Computer Game Update*. (Only $16 for a 12-issue subscription; send your check to Circuit City, P.O. Box 240523, Honolulu, HI, 96824-0523. How's that for a blatant plug?)
- Thanks to Kathy Mejia for proofreading the text in this book. I promise I'll make more typos next time Kathy—not!
- Thanks to my uncle, Ted Tesman, for his financial advice.
- Last, and definitely not least, thanks to my Mom for giving me more love than any son deserves. I'll be your baby elf forever, Mom.

Contents

#

Introduction

(Author's Note: Throughout most of the book, I've referred to The Legend of Zelda: A Link to the Past video game with the acronym LTP [**L**ink **T**o the **P**ast]. This saves me from the unenviable task of having to type "The Legend of Zelda: A Link to the Past video game" a zillion times.)

A (VERY) BRIEF HISTORY OF ZELDA

The Legend of Zelda is arguably the greatest adventure game of all time. Released for the Nintendo Entertainment System in 1987, it has entertained millions of players with its perfect combination of tricky puzzles and arcade action. It's not surprising to learn that the designer of The Legend of Zelda, Shigeru Miyamoto, also came up with Super Mario Bros., which was bundled with the NES and was largely responsible for its sales success.

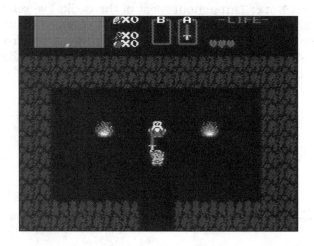

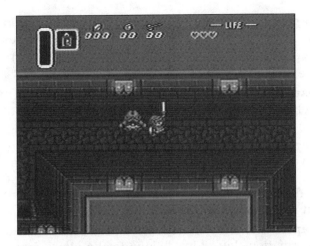

Like most popular video games, The Legend of Zelda spawned a sequel: Zelda II: The Adventure of Link. The sequel was certainly entertaining, but most players agreed that it lacked the "spark" of the original game.

The Legend of Zelda: A Link to the Past is a 16-bit continuation of the Zelda game series. Most players refer to it as Zelda III, but that's not the game's official title, and Nintendo of America Inc. states that they may yet release a true Zelda III video game for the 8-bit NES. (After the 16-bit intensity of LTP, however, it's doubtful that many players would care much about another 8-bit Zelda game.)

HOW TO USE THIS BOOK

This book is divided into nine chapters of information that will answer any question, solve any problem, and turn your frown upside-down.

Chapter 1 is all about **Bosses** and how to beat them.

Chapter 2 details the **Dungeons** with complete maps and detailed text that tells where to find important objects, how to open the doors in certain rooms, and how to get into hard-to-reach rooms.

Chapter 3 talks about those darling li'l **Faeries** and their locations in the Light and Dark Worlds.

Chapter 4 spills the beans on the **Heart Containers** by revealing how to collect all 24 (!) Heart Container Pieces.

Chapter 5 is a complete guide to the **Items** in LTP: where they are, how to get them, and what to do with them.

Chapter 6 takes you to the major **Locations** in LTP, and also helpfully explains just why the heck you should visit them.

Chapter 7 is a **Walkthrough** to LTP with a sadistic twist: it tells you what to do, but not how to do it. You have to refer to other chapters (or figure it out yourself) if you're stuck on how to do something. This way, you can use the Walkthrough without completely spoiling LTP.

Chapter 8 is full of **Weird, Wild Stuff:** miscellaneous tips and information that didn't belong in the other chapters. It's fun just to browse through this chapter and try some of the goofy tricks detailed therein.

Chapter 9 covers **Link's Awakening** for the Game Boy. This complete walkthrough will help you figure out what to do and how to do it.

HOW TO USE THE MAPS

At the end of this introduction, you'll find two maps of the Light World and Dark World. (These maps are the same ones that appear when you press the X button during the game.) The maps have been divided into eight-by-eight grids.

Whenever I refer to a particular location in this book, I use a coordinate system to tell you where the location is found on either of the maps. For example, here are the coordinates for Link's House:

L-E6/N

L indicates the Light World.
E6 indicates the square on the Light World map.
N indicates the north section of the square.

Here's another example coordinate for the Blacksmith's House:

D-C4/SE

D indicates the Dark World.
C4 indicates the square on the Dark World map.
SE indicates the southeast section of the square.

So, when you read a coordinate, here's what you're seeing:

X-YY/ZZ

X is the World. L=Light World, D=Dark World. If this letter is missing, that's because it's obvious which World the coordinates apply to. (For example, in the list of "Dark World Large Faeries" in Chapter 3, you won't see this letter.)
YY is the map square.
ZZ is the section of the map square. NW=Northwest, N=North, NE=Northeast, W=West, C=Center, E=East, SW=Southwest, S=South, SE=Southeast.

Obviously, this coordinate system isn't exact, but it'll get you where you need to go with a minimum of fuss. Keep referring to the Full World and Close Up Maps when you're headed somewhere and compare your location to your destination coordinates. After a bit of practice, you'll be negotiating the land of Hyrule like a pro.

THE ADVENTURE BEGINS...

You've finished reading this chapter. You know a little bit about The Legend of Zelda. You know how this book is organized. And you know how to use the maps. You're ready for action. Read on and have fun!

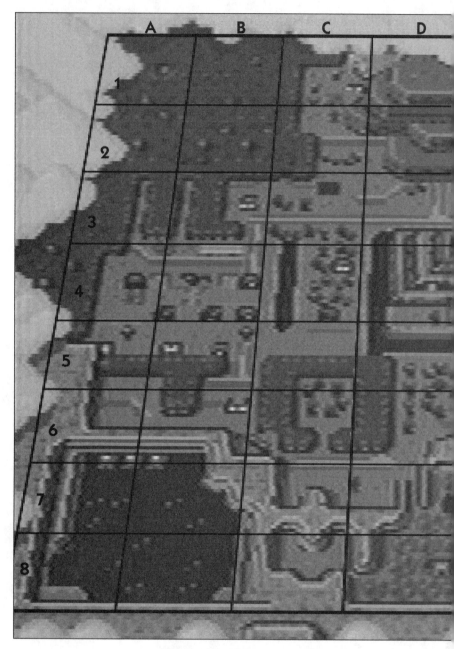

DARK WORLD

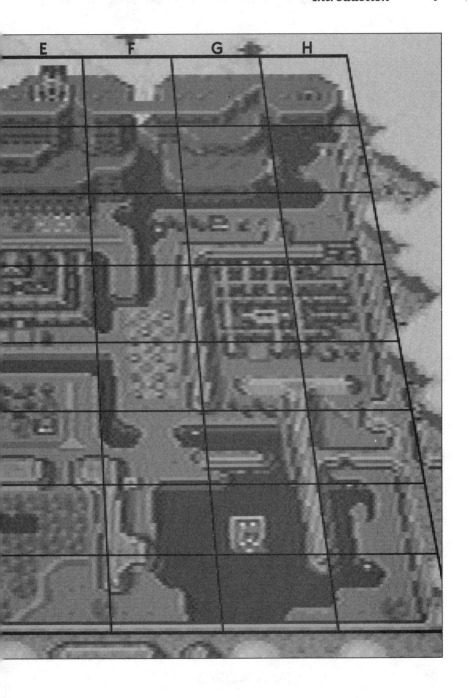

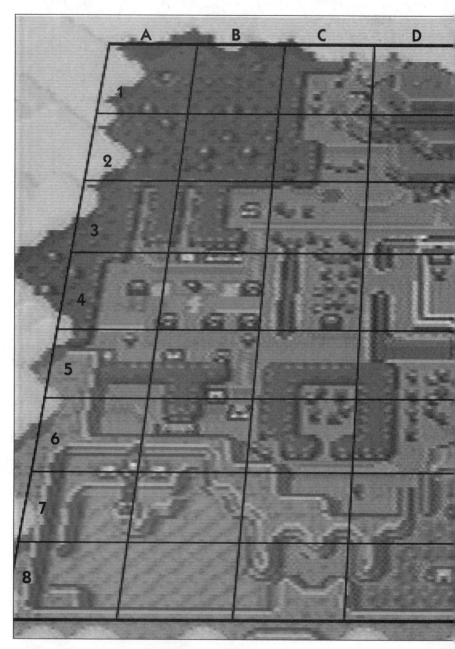

LIGHT WORLD

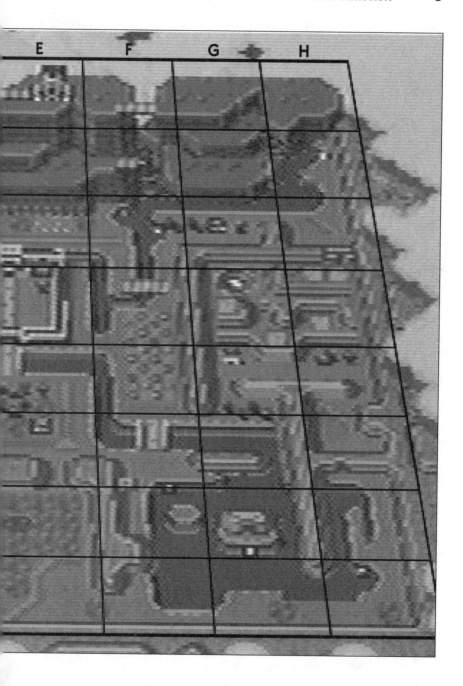

Bosses

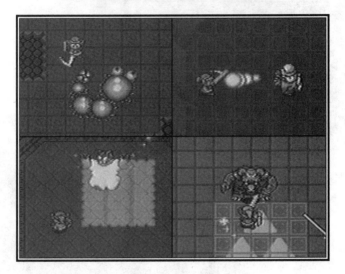

INTRODUCTION

There are fourteen Bosses in LTP, from the laughably wimpy Ball and Chain Trooper to the mighty Ganon. A Heart Container appears after you defeat eleven of the Bosses. The only three Bosses that don't give you Containers are Agahnim and Ganon. (You fight Agahnim twice, so he counts as two Bosses.) We've listed the Bosses in the order you fight them when using the Walkthrough in Chapter 7, although you're almost guaranteed to encounter them in this order whether you use the Walkthrough or not.

LIGHT WORLD BOSSES

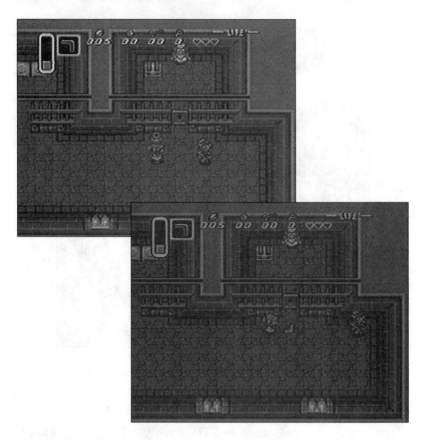

Hyrule Castle (Rescuing Zelda):
Ball and Chain Trooper

There are two ways to take out the Trooper. Stun him with the Blue Boomerang and whack him with your Sword, or pick up the jars in the empty cell and hurl them at the Trooper. Either method does the trick.

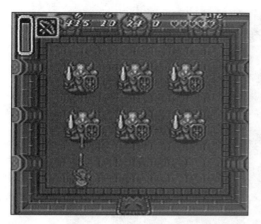

Eastern Palace: Armos Knights

Stand in a corner and shoot the Knights with your Bow. It takes three Arrows to destroy each Knight. If you run out of Arrows, use your Sword. When you've destroyed all but one of the Knights, the final Knight starts moving around rapidly. Keep moving and remember that you can hit the last Knight whether he's on the ground or in the air.

Desert Palace: Lanmolas

Whenever a Lanmola bursts out of the ground, stand above, below, or to either side to avoid the rocks caused by the bursting. Use the Spin Attack to hit the Lanmolas in the head. You can also use your Bow, but the Spin Attack does far more damage. The last Lanmola kicks out rocks in eight directions, making it harder to dodge them.

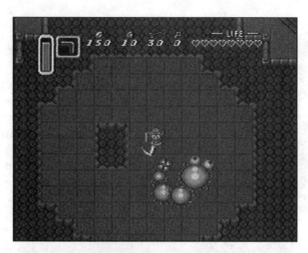

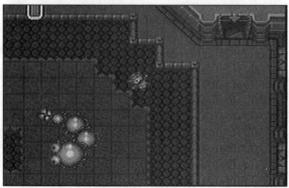

Tower of Hera: Moldorm

Use the Spin Attack to hit the Moldorm in the tail. If you fall off the platform, or through the hole in the middle of the platform, you'll have to climb back up and once again battle the Moldorm—and it regains all of its energy when you fall.

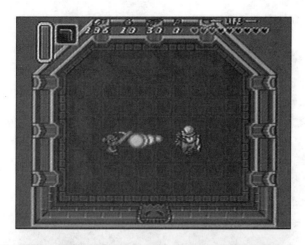

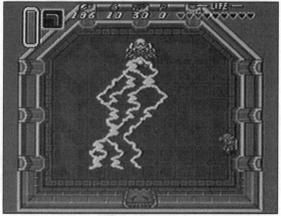

Hyrule Castle (Climbing to Agahnim): Agahnim

Use the Master Sword or Bug-Catching Net to reflect Agahnim's energy balls back at him. If Agahnim appears at the top and middle of the screen, move to one side to avoid his lightning attack.

DARK WORLD BOSSES

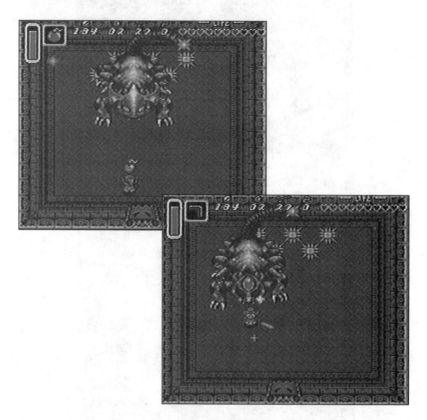

Level 1 (Dark Palace): Helmasaur King

Throw Bombs at the King's mask to blow it open. (You can also drop Bombs in the Helmasaur's path and hope he walks into them.) If you don't want to use Bombs, or don't have any, use the Magic Hammer to chip away at the mask. Once you've destroyed the mask, use the Spin Attack to hit the green jewel in the King's head. If the King's tail starts moving rapidly, run into the lower-left or lower-right corner to dodge.

Level 2 (Swamp Palace): Arrghus

Use the Hookshot to pull the Arrghi creatures away from
Arrghus and kill them with your Sword. When all the little
Arrghi are destroyed, attack Arrghus with your Sword.

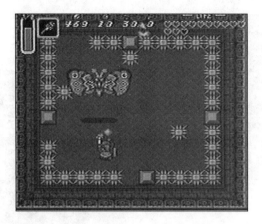

Level 3 (Skull Palace): Mothula

Dodge the spikes and shoot Mothula with the Fire Rod. Use your Sword when you run out of Magic Power.

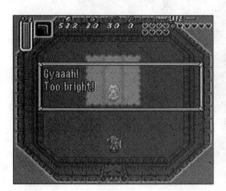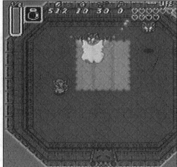

Level 4 (Gargoyle's Domain): Blind the Thief

Go to the easternmost room on Floor F1 and throw a Bomb at the crack on the floor to create a hole. Go down to Floor B1 and rescue the maiden, then take her to the Boss's room (indicated by the flashing skull on the map). Lead her into the sunlight and she turns into Blind. Hit Blind with the Spin Attack and ignore the flying heads, since you can't damage them.

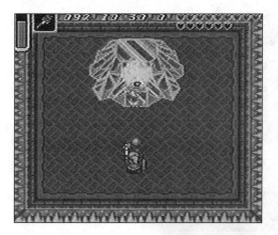

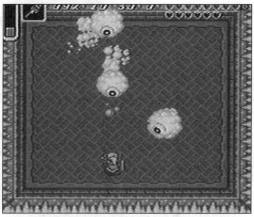

Level 5 (Ice Island): Kholdstare

Shoot the ice shield with the Fire Rod eight times to break it
open, then attack the three eyeballs with the Fire Rod and
Sword while dodging the falling ice balls.

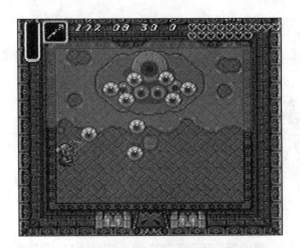

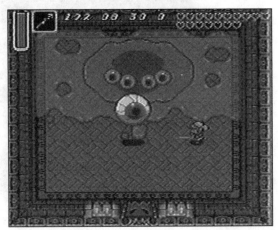

Level 6 (Misery Maze): Vitreous

Stand on one side of the room and smack away the eyeballs with your Sword. Keep destroying the eyeballs until there are only four left and Vitreous pulls itself out of the slime to attack you. Hit Vitreous with the Spin Attack.

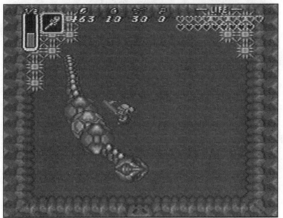

Level 7 (Turtle Rock): Trinexx

Shoot Trinexx's left head with the Ice Rod and destroy it with the Sword. (Don't use the Spin Attack, just hack away.) Shoot Trinexx's right head with the Fire Rod and use Sword swings to destroy it. When both heads have been destroyed, Trinexx turns into a long snakelike creature. Hit Trinexx in the midsection with the Spin Attack.

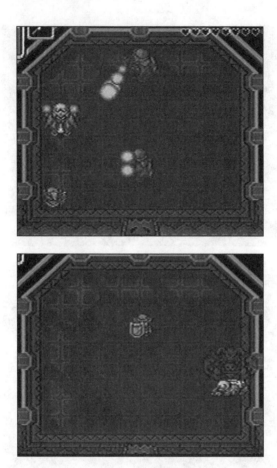

Level 8 (Ganon's Tower): Agahnim

In your second battle, Agahnim attacks with two "clones" of
himself. The fake Agahnims are easy to spot, since they're
hazy and transparent. Use the Sword or Bug-Catching Net to
deflect Agahnim's energy balls back at him. Agahnim doesn't
attack with lightning this time, so don't worry about having to
dodge that particular attack.

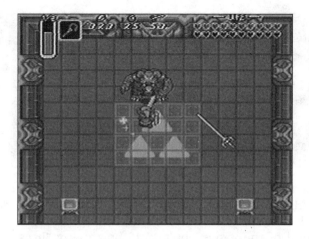

Pyramid of Power: Ganon

Use the Cane of Byrna or the Magic Cape to make yourself invincible, and attack Ganon continuously. Make sure you don't fall off the edge of the platform. If you do, walk back outside, climb back to the top of the Pyramid, and jump into the hole to try again.

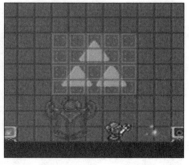

When Ganon says "En Garde!", make the Fire Rod your active item. When the torches go out, use the Fire Rod to light them back up. Hit Ganon with your Sword to make him turn blue, and shoot him with a Silver Arrow to cause damage.

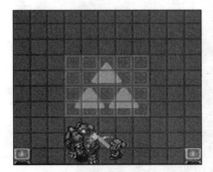 

Shoot fast, because he doesn't stay blue for long. Four Silver Arrows kill Ganon once and for all. Walk through the door to the north and enjoy the nine-minute-long (!) ending sequence. At the end of the game, you're told how many "lives" it took you to complete LTP; the amount is even recorded on your saved game. (Don't ask how high our number was the first time we finished ...)

Dungeons

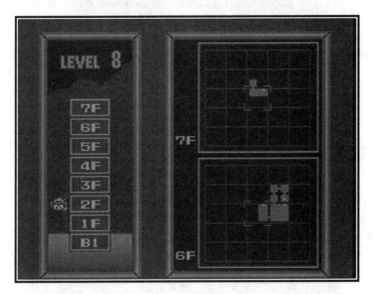

INTRODUCTION

They're deep, dark, and teeming with evil. They're the dungeons of Hyrule, and you're gonna have to hack and slash your way through every one of them to win the game.

In this chapter, you'll find maps for every dungeon, lists of the locations of important items, and solutions to the trickier puzzles. You'll also find a list of things to try when you just can't seem to make any more progress in a dungeon. Read on!

WHEN IN DOUBT...

It's easy to get stuck in a dungeon, unable to make any progress because you can't find a Key or figure out how to open a door. Here are some things to try.

- Kill all of the monsters in a room. Monsters sometimes have Keys in their possession, and doors sometimes open when all of the monsters in a room have been eliminated.
- Search for hidden buttons and floor switches. Pick up everything you can and you may find a hidden button. Floor switches are harder to see, since they look very similar to the normal floor tiles.
- In a room with floating floor tiles, dodge the tiles until they stop popping out of the floor. The door(s) may open.
- In rooms with large gaps in the floor, use the Hookshot to swing across.

HYRULE CASTLE (RESCUING ZELDA)

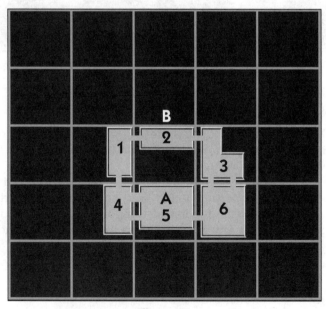

Floor 1F

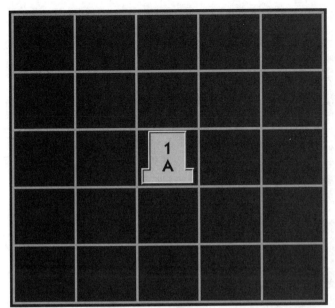

Floor 2F

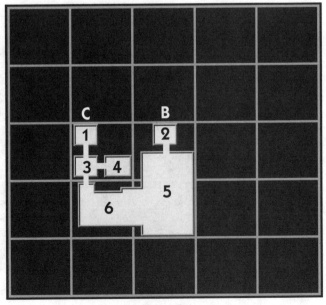

Floor B1

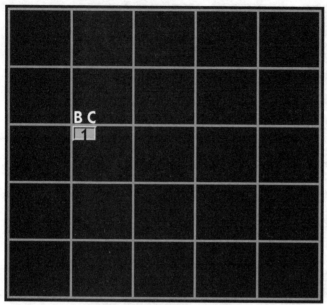

Floor B2

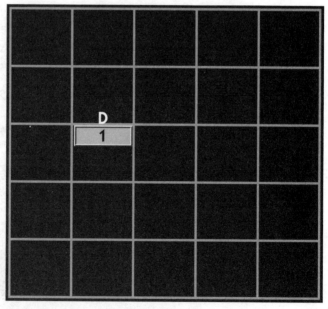

Floor B3

Getting Inside

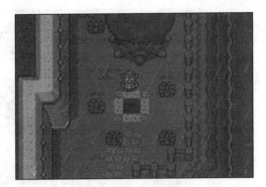

At the start of the game, when your Uncle leaves the house, jump out of bed and open the chest to collect the Lamp. Go outside and walk north to Hyrule Castle. Cross the bridge, then follow the path leading to the east. Pull up the bush at the end of the path and jump into the hole.

The Map

Open the chest in Room B1-2.

The Blue Boomerang

Open the chest in Room B1-4.

Beating the Boss (Ball and Chain Trooper)

There are two ways to take out the Trooper. Stun him with the Blue Boomerang and whack him with your Sword, or pick up the jars in the empty cell and hurl them at the Trooper. Either method does the trick.

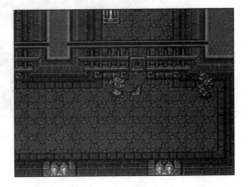

Room 2F-1: A Secret Path

Come to this room with Princess Zelda and push the ornamental shelf from the left to reveal a secret passage to Sanctuary.

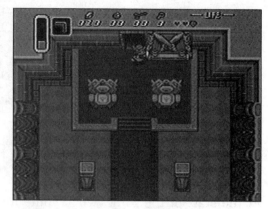

HYRULE CASTLE (ESCAPING TO SANCTUARY)

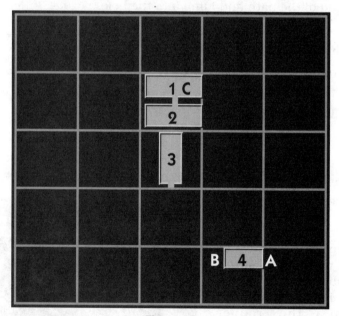

Floor 1F

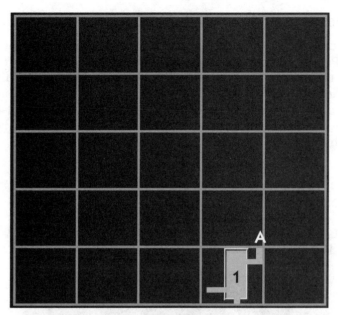

Floor 2F

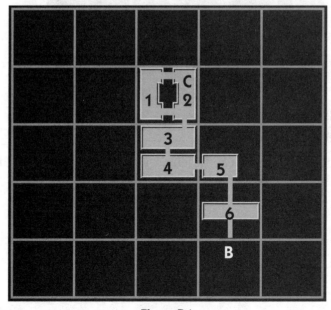

Floor B1

Rooms B1-1, B1-2: No Entry

You can't bash through the cracks into Room 1 until you get the Pegasus Shoes later in the game. Once you have them, visit the Graveyard and push the northwest stone. Drop into the hole and you'll fall into Room B1-2. Dash Attack either of the cracks, or use a Bomb, and enter Room 1. You'll find three chests filled with goodies (but nothing necessary to finish the game).

Room 1F-2: Which Switch?

Pull the switch on the left and a group of snakes drops into the room. Pull the switch on the right and you'll open the door to Sanctuary.

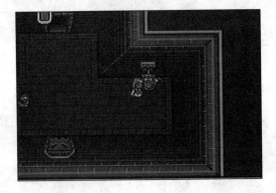

Room 1F-3: Sanctuary

Talk to the Sage, open the chest for a Heart Container, then go outside and head for Kakariko Village.

EASTERN PALACE (L-H3/S)

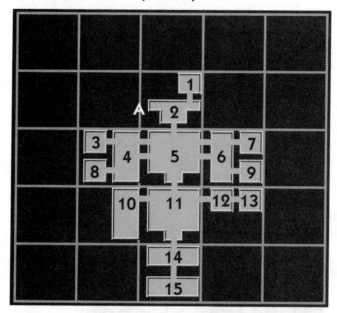

Floor 1F

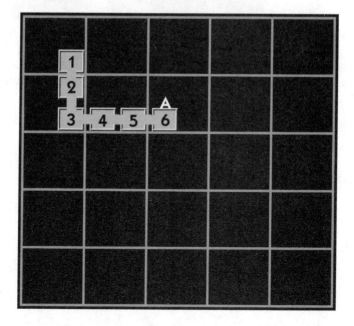

Floor 2F

Major Enemies

Goriyas: These ratlike creatures come in two Christmasy colors, green and red. The green Goriyas can be killed with Sword strokes, but the only way to kill a Red Goriya is with Arrows. Goriyas move in the opposite direction that you move in.

The Big Key

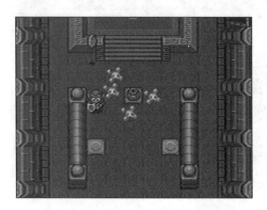

Go to Room 1F-10. There's a jar in the middle of the room surrounded by four Fire Faeries. Defeat all of the enemies in the room and the Faeries spin off the jar. Pick up the jar to reveal a button. Walk onto the button to make a hidden chest appear on the blue pedestal. Open the chest for the Big Key.

The Compass

Open the chest in Room 1F-3.

The Map

Go to Room 1F-7, then go north into Room 1F-9 and open the chest.

The Big Chest (Bow)

Open the Big Chest in Room 1F-5.

Beating the Boss (Armos Knights)

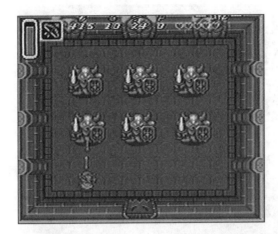

Stand in a corner and shoot the Knights with your Bow. It takes three Arrows to destroy each Knight. If you run out of Arrows, use your Sword. When you've destroyed all but one of the Knights, the final Knight starts moving around rapidly. Keep moving and remember that you can hit the last Knight whether he's on the ground or in the air.

Room 1F-1: Rupee Riches

This room is filled with blue Rupees and two Fire Faeries guarding them.

Room 1F-5: Hidden Faeries

See those large jars next to the north door? Jump off either of the ledges below the door and fall into a jar. You'll appear in a hidden room with two Fire Faeries.

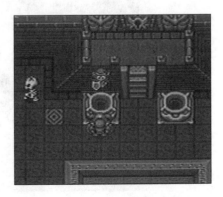

DESERT PALACE (L-A7/NE)

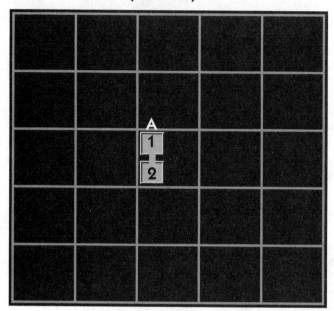

Floor 1F

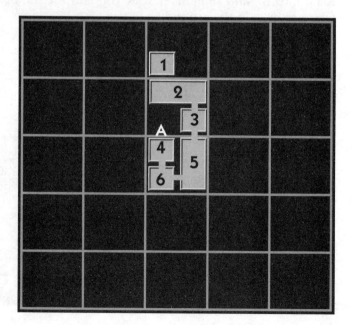

Floor 2F

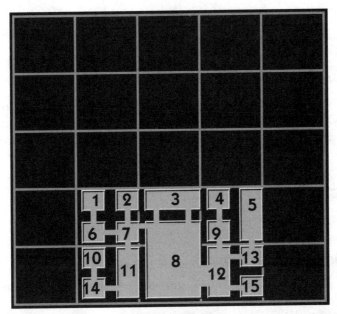

Floor B1

Getting Inside

Use the Book of Mudora to read the monument in front of the Desert Palace.

Major Enemies

Statue Sentries: These pillars scan the room in a circle and blast at you with powerful

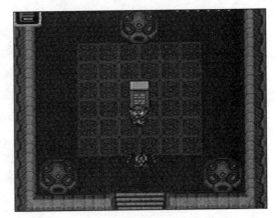

lasers. Stay ahead of, or behind, the circular scan.

The Big Key

Go to the north end of Room 1B-5 and open the chest.

The Compass

Go to Room 1B-13 and open the chest.

The Map

Go to Room 1B-3. Pick up the jar between the two green Goriyas to reveal a button. Walk onto the button to make a hidden chest appear between the torches. Open the chest for the Map.

The Big Chest (Power Glove)

Open the Big Chest in Room B1-1.

Beating the Boss (Lanmolas)

Whenever a Lanmola bursts out of the ground, stand above, below, or to either side to avoid the rocks caused by the bursting. Use the Spin Attack to hit the Lanmolas in the head. You can also use your Bow, but the Spin Attack does

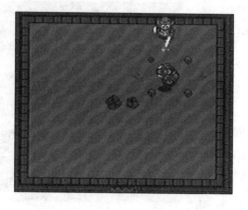

far more damage. The last Lanmola kicks out rocks in eight directions, making it harder to dodge them.

Floor 1F: Where's the Door?

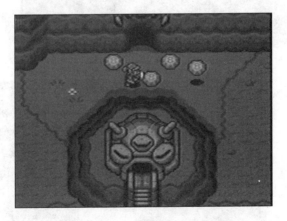

After exploring Floor B1 and finding the Power Glove, use the southwest or southeast exit and walk north of the Palace to find a cave surrounded by rocks. Pick up the rocks and go into the cave, which is the entrance to Room 1F-2.

Room 2F-2: Four Torches

Light the four torches to cause the walls to slide back and reveal a door.

TOWER OF HERA (L-E1/N)

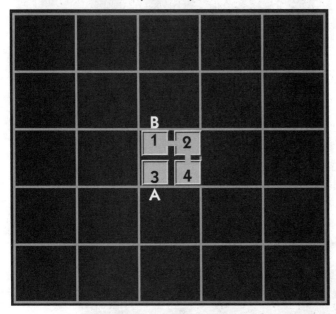

Floor 1F

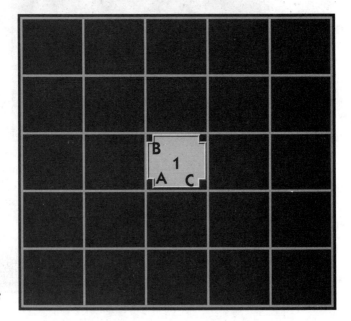

Floor 2F

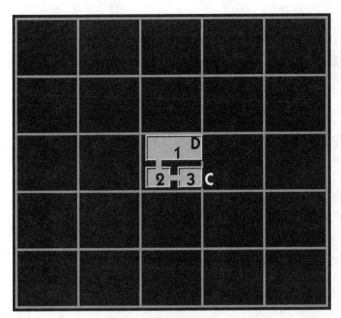

Floor 3F

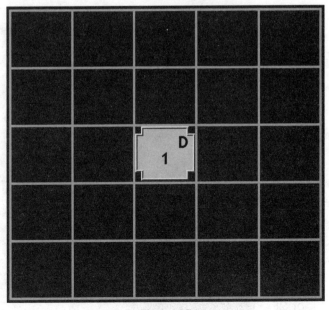

Floor 4F

Floor 5F

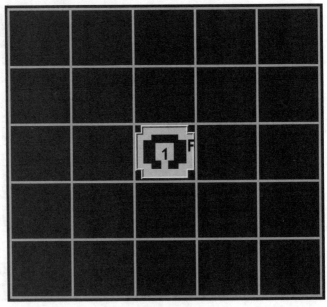

Floor 6F

Getting Inside

Go through the caves of Death Mountain and walk to the Warp Tile east of Spectacle Rock. Walk onto the Tile to warp into the Dark World. Walk west and stand in the middle of the spectacle shape on the

ground, then use the Magic Mirror to return to the Light World. You'll appear on top of Spectacle Rock. Walk north to jump off the Rock, then walk east to the Tower.

The Big Key

Go to Room 1F-4 and light the four torches to make a hidden chest appear. Open the chest for the Big Key.

The Compass

Go to Room 4F-1 and open the chest.

The Map

Go to the north end of Room 2F-1 and open the chest.

The Big Chest (Moon Pearl)

Walk up to Room 5F-1 and walk onto the Star Tile to make a hole appear in the middle of the room. Drop into the hole and you'll land in front of the Big Chest.

Beating the Boss (Moldorm)

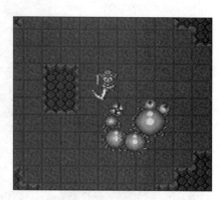

Use the Spin Attack to hit the Moldorm in the tail. If you fall off the platform, or through the hole in the middle of the platform, you'll have to climb back up and once again battle the Moldorm—and it regains all of its energy when you fall.

Room 5F-1: Hidden Faeries

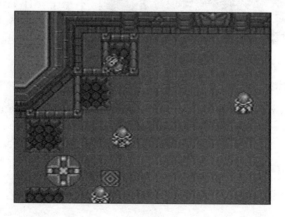

Drop through the hole in the northwest corner of the room (next to the crack in the wall). You'll fall several floors into a hidden room with two Small Faeries. The Warp Tile takes you back to Room 5F-1.

HYRULE CASTLE (CLIMBING TO AGAHNIM)

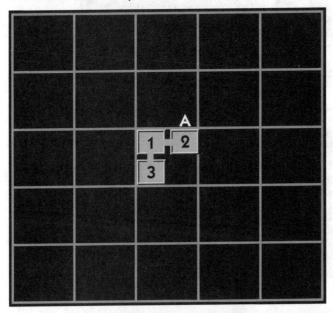

Floor 2F

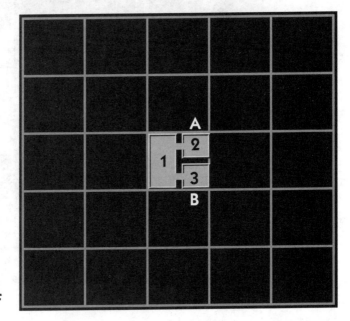

Floor 3F

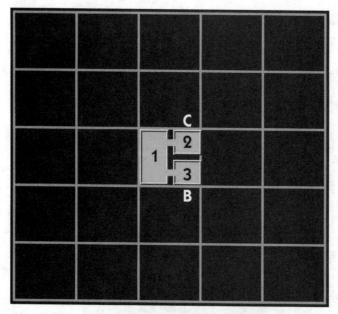

Floor 4F

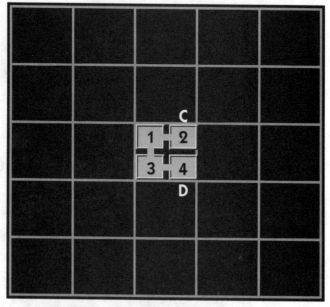

Floor 5F

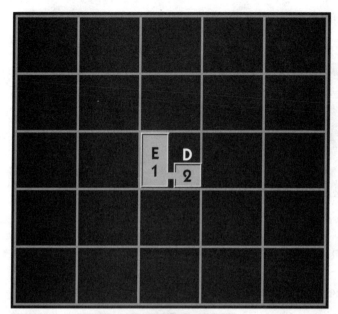

Floor 6F

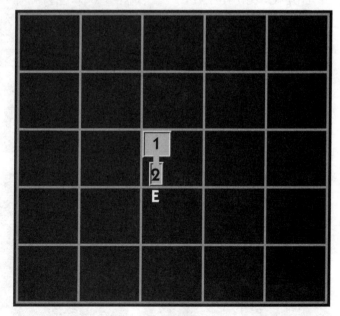

Floor 7F

Getting Inside

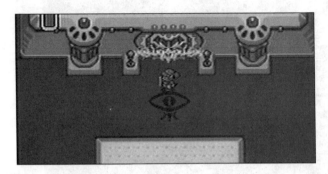

Walk to Hyrule Castle and climb up to Floor 1F. Find the door blocked by a strange beam of light. Swing your Master Sword at the beam to destroy it and walk through the door.

Beating the Boss (Agahnim)

Use the Master Sword or Bug-Catching Net to reflect Agahnim's energy balls back at him. If Agahnim appears at the top and middle of the screen, move to one side to avoid his lightning attack.

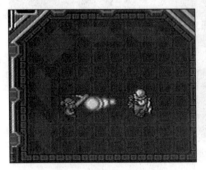

DARK PALACE (D-H3/S)

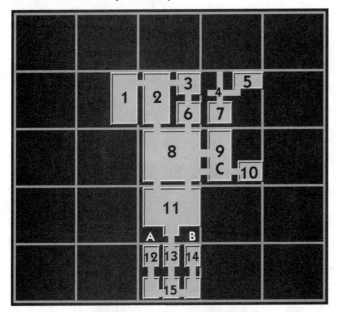

Floor 1F

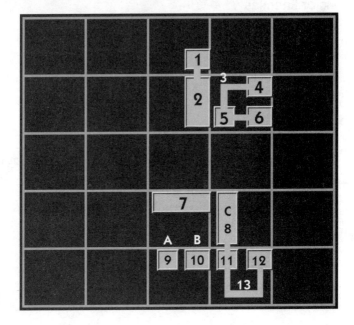

Floor B1

Getting Inside

In one of the grassy mazes outside the Dark Palace, you'll meet up with Kiki the Monkey. Pay him 10 Rupees to follow you and walk to the entrance of the Dark Palace. Don't get hit by an enemy or Kiki will run back to the maze, and you'll have to go get him back (paying another 10 Rupees to do so). At the entrance, Kiki will offer to open the door for 100 more Rupees. Pay him the bucks and watch him pop the door open.

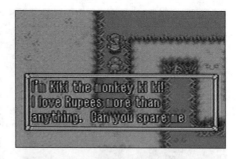

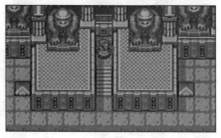

Major Enemies

Helmasaurs: These little buggers have hard heads. Attack them from behind to defeat them.

Moles: These red and blue creatures pop in and out of the ground, blocking your progress. Flatten them with the Magic Hammer.

The Big Key

Walk onto the west walkway in Room 1F-12. Plant a Bomb on the crack in the walkway to blow a hole through. Drop into the hole and into Room B1-7. Walk north and open the door (you'll need a Key), then walk up the stairs to the Chest with the Big Key inside.

The Compass

Open the chest in Room 1F-3.

The Map

Go to Room B1-10 and walk onto the Warp Tile. You'll appear in Room B1-12. Make your way to Room B1-8 and walk up the stairs to Room 1F-10. Open the chest for the Map.

The Big Chest (Magic Hammer)

Run along the bridge in Room 1F-2 before it starts to collapse, then go through the west door into Room 1F-1. (You'll need a Key to unlock the door.) Make your way to the east side of the room and Bomb through the crack in the wall. Walk through the hole to the Big Chest.

Beating the Boss (Helmasaur King)

Throw Bombs at the King's mask to blow it open. (You can also drop Bombs in the Helmasaur's path and hope he walks into them.) If you don't want to use Bombs, or don't have any, use the Magic Hammer to chip away at the mask. Once you've destroyed the mask, use the Spin Attack to hit the green jewel in the King's head. If the King's tail starts moving rapidly, run into the lower-left or lower-right corner to dodge.

Room 1F-9: Button Pushing

Pick up the skulls in the northeast corner of the room to find a button. Push the upper-right statue onto the button to hold open the north door.

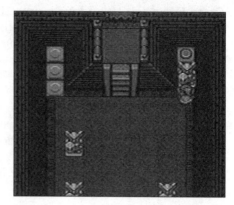

Room 1F-4: Shoot To Kill

Shoot the green statue in the eye with an Arrow to reveal Room 1F-5.

SWAMP PALACE (D-D8/E)

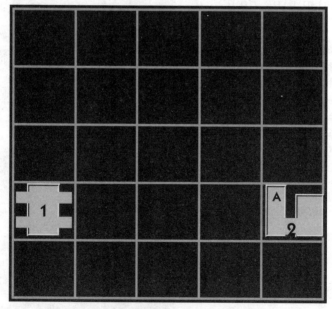

Floor 1F

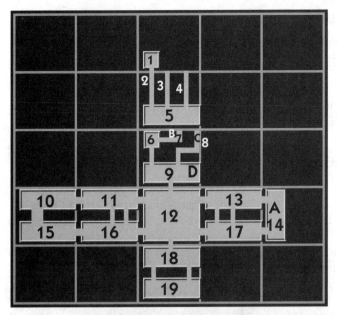

Floor B1

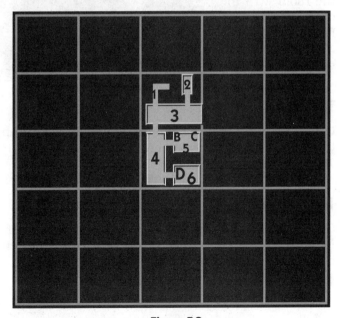

Floor B2

Getting Inside

Enter the Watergate at L-D8/E and walk north to the switches. Pull the switch on the right to open the dam and drain the water in the Great Swamp. Walk outside and use the Magic Mirror to warp to the Dark World. Go into the Swamp Palace and you'll be able to swim to the stairs going down to Floor B1.

Major Enemies

Switches: These items aren't exactly dangerous, but you'll have to find and trip them to progress into the Palace. If you can't get through a room because of an out-of-reach ladder, look for a Switch and push it from the right to turn it on and release a flow of water. Return to the room with the out-of-reach ladder and you'll now be able to swim right to it.

The Big Key

Go to Room B1-15 and climb up to Room 1F-2. Drop through the hole in the northeast corner of the room into Room B1-10. Walk east into Room B1-11 and open the chest.

The Compass

Go into Room B1-18 and use the southeast door to enter Room B1-19. Walk through the room and use the northwest door to go back into Room B1-18. Open the chest.

The Map

Go to Room B1-14 and Bomb through the crack in the northwest corner. Walk through the hole into Room B1-13 and open the chest.

The Big Chest (Hookshot)

Go to Room B1-12 and open the Big Chest.

Beating the Boss (Arrghus)

Use the Hookshot to pull the Arrghi creatures away from Arrghus and kill them with your Sword. When all the little Arrghi are destroyed, attack Arrghus with your Sword.

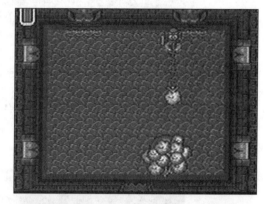

Room B1-9: Button Pushing and Switch Hitting

Pick up the jar in the northwest corner to reveal a button, then push the statue onto the button to hold open the doors into

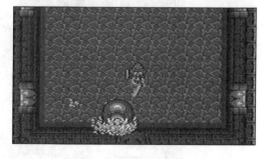

Rooms B1-6 and B1-8. Go into Room B1-8 and climb down the stairs to Room B2-5. Hit the switch to drain the room and open the way into the rest of the Palace.

Room B1-12: Hard-to-Find Key

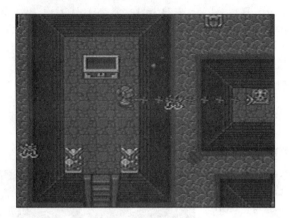

Stand just below the Big Chest and use the Hookshot to latch onto the skull on the east side of the room. Swing across and pick up the skull against the wall to find a Key.

SKULL PALACE

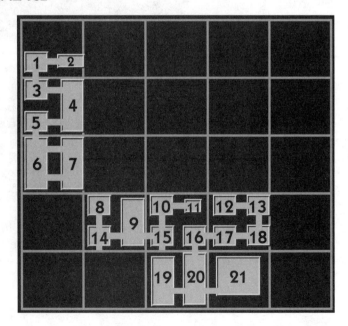

Floor B1

Floor B2

Getting Inside

There are eight entrances to the Skull Palace, scattered throughout the Skull Woods. Six of the entrances are easy to find, but two of them aren't.

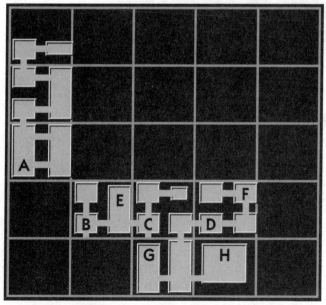

This map of the Skull Palace is labeled with the eight entrances from the Skull Woods.

Entrance A:
You can't get
inside until you
have the Fire Rod.
Use the Rod to
burn away
the front of the
large skull.

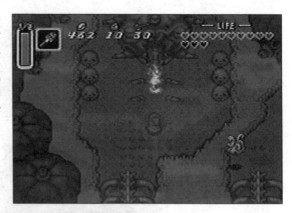

Entrance F:
Chop down the 3x3
cluster of bushes to
find the entrance.

Major Enemies

Gibdos: These bandaged buggers can take a lot of punishment from your Sword. The best way to dispose of them is with the Fire Rod.

The Big Key

Use Entrance C to walk into Room B1-15. Pick up the skull below the door to reveal a button. Pull the statue on the right onto the button. Stay above the statue so you can walk through the north door, into Room B1-10, once the statue is on the button. Open the chest in Room B1-10.

The Compass

Use Entrance G to fall into Room B1-19. Go into Room B1-20 and open the chest.

The Map

Use Entrance H to fall into Room B1-21. Go into Room B1-18 and walk onto the Star Tile, then open the chest.

The Big Chest (Fire Rod)

Use Entrance F to fall into Room B1-13. Bomb through the west wall and go into Room B1-12. Pull the switch to blow up the wall between this room and Room B1-17. Go into Room B1-17 and open the Big Chest.

Beating the Boss (Mothula)

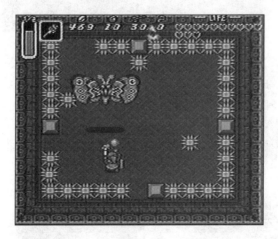

Dodge the spikes and shoot Mothula with the Fire Rod. Use your Sword when you run out of Magic Power.

GARGOYLE'S DOMAIN (D/B4-C)

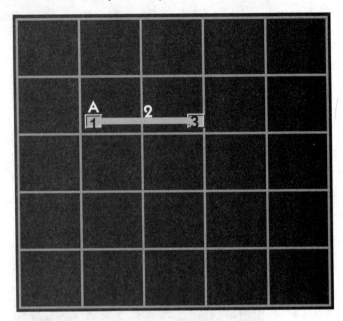

Floor 1F

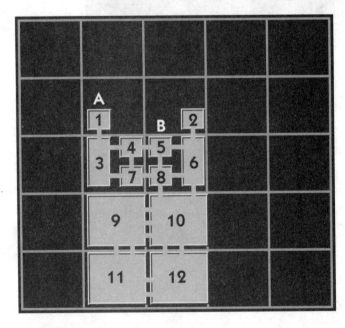

Floor B1

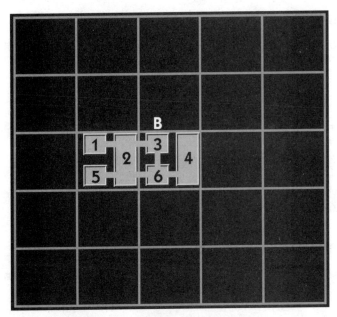

Floor B2

Getting Inside

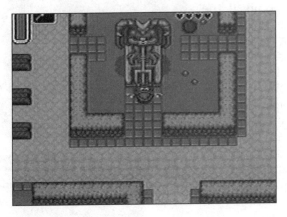

Pull on the gargoyle statue's pitchfork until it blows up. Easy.

The Big Key

Go to Room B1-12 and walk through the southwest passage into Room B1-11. Open the chest.

The Compass

Go to Room B1-12 and open the chest.

The Map

Walk into the northwest corner of Room B1-11 and open the chest.

The Big Chest (Titan's Mitt)

Go to Room B2-5 and use the Magic Hammer to flatten the Moles, then open the Big Chest.

Beating the Boss (Blind the Thief)

Go to Room 1F-3 and throw a bomb at the crack on the floor to create a hole. (See below.) Go down to Room B2-4 and rescue the maiden, then take her to Room B1-2. Lead her into the sunlight and she turns into Blind.

Hit Blind with the Spin Attack and ignore the flying heads, since you can't damage them.

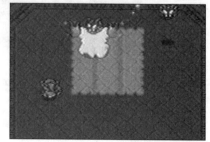

Room 1F-3: See the Light

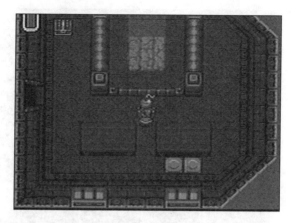

Plant a Bomb, pick it up, and throw it onto the crack beneath the window. When the Bomb explodes, a beam of light will shine through the hole and into Room B1-2.

Room B2-4: Damsel in Distress (Not!)

The Maiden in Room B2-4 may seem like a harmless gal, but she's actually Blind the Thief. Take her to Room B1-2 (after blowing up the floor in Room 1F-3) and lead her into the light to cause Blind to shed his disguise.

ICE ISLAND (D-G7/C)

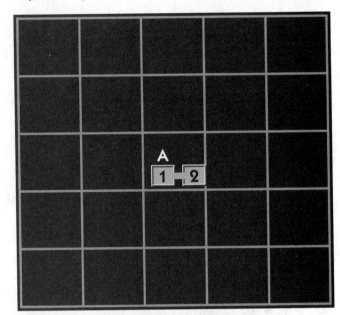

Floor 1F

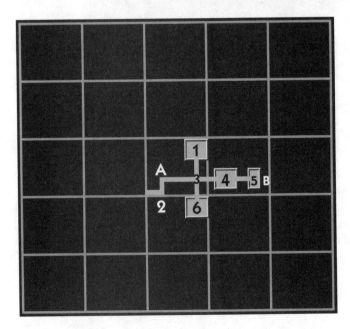

Floor B1

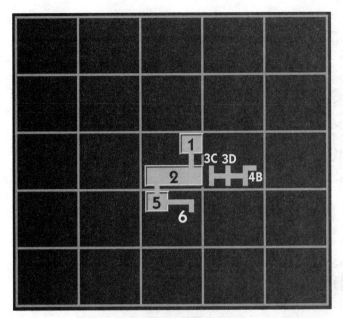

Floor B2

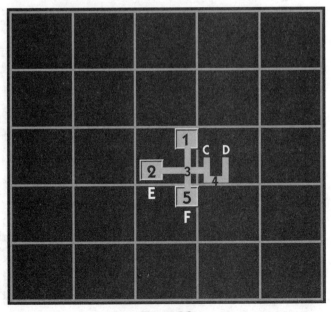

Floor B3

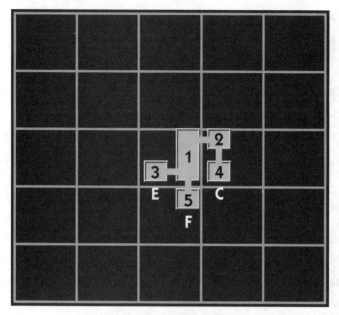

Floor B4

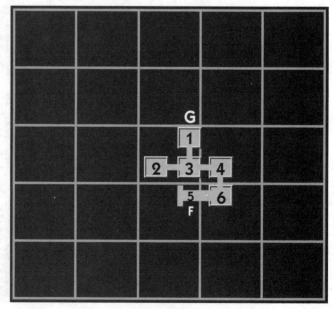

Floor B5

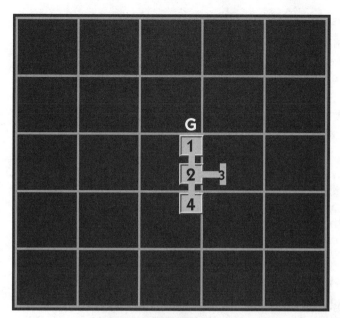

Floor B6

Floor B7

Getting Inside

Walk to the entrance of the Pond of Happiness at L-G7/C. Pick up the heavy rock to reveal a Warp Tile. Walk onto the Tile and you'll appear in the Dark World, inside the walls of Ice Island.

Major Enemies

Pentagors: These psycho penguins can be eliminated with a single hit from the Hookshot.

Stalfos Knights: You can defeat the Knights with roughly a zillion Sword blows, but there's a much easier way. Hit a Knight with your Sword and he collapses into a pile of bones. Drop a Bomb on him and he's history.

The Big Key

Immediately after collecting the Map (see below), pull the tongue of the statue to open the east door. Go to Room B2-4 and climb up to Room B1-5. Open the chest.

The Compass

Go to Room B1-6 and defeat all of the Pentagors to make a chest appear. Open the chest.

The Map

Go to Room B3-4 and climb up the stairs in the northeast corner to Room B2-3. Pick up the skulls and walk onto the button to make a hidden chest appear. Open the chest.

The Big Chest (Blue Mail)

Go to Room B3-2 and climb down the stairs to Room B4-3. Drop a Bomb on the cracks above the stairs to create a hole, then drop through the hole into Room B5-2. Open the Big Chest.

Beating the Boss (Kholdstare)

Shoot the ice shield with the Fire Rod eight times to break it open, then at-tack the three eyeballs with the Fire Rod and Sword while dodging the falling ice balls.

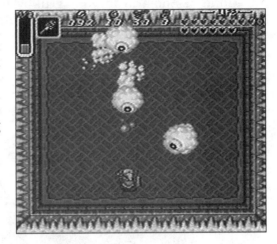

Room B1-1: Stupid Bomb Tricks

Hit the Crystal Switch to lower the blue walls, then drop a Bomb next to the Switch and walk to the north end of the room. When the Bomb explodes, the Switch lowers the orange walls. Bomb through the crack in the floor and drop to Floor B2.

Room B4-2: Hard to Cross

Use the Hookshot to swing across the gap by latching onto the ice blocks.

Room B6-2: Button Pushing

Go to Room B6-3 and hit the Crystal Switch to lower the blue walls, then follow this path: west to B6-2, north to B6-1, up to B5-1, south to B5-3, east to B5-4, south to B5-6, west to B5-5, up to B4-5, north to B4-1, west to B4-3. Once you reach B4-3, drop through the hole into Room B5-2 and walk east into Room B5-3. Push the lower-left ice block into the hole, then drop through the hole into Room B6-2. Push the ice block onto the button to hold the south door open.

If you go to the Misery Maze before coming here, and have the Cane of Somaria in your grubby little paws, create a Somarian block and push it onto the button to keep the door open.

MISERY MAZE (D-A7/NW)

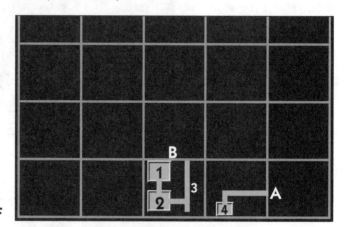

Floor 1F

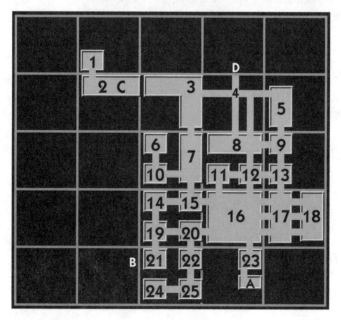

Floor B1

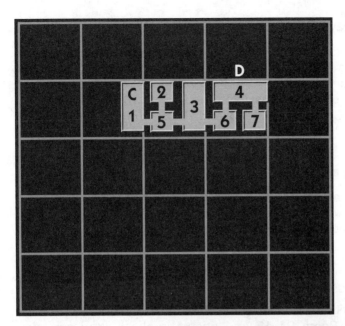

Floor B2

Getting Inside

Stand on the Ether Medallion symbol and use the Ether Medallion. You'll clear up the weather in the Misery Mire and create the entrance to Misery Maze.

Major Enemies

Wizzrobe: This magical dude fades in and out of the screen, shooting lightning bolts at you. Strike him as soon as he appears, before he can shoot at you.

The Big Key

Go to Rooms 1F-1 and 1F-2. Push through the blocks in the two rooms so that you can reach the four torches, but don't light them yet. Once you have access to all four torches, light them as quickly as possible. The screen will shake for a few seconds. Go to Room 1F-3 and drop through the hole into Room B1-25. Open the chest.

The Compass

Go to Room B1-19. Light the four torches to open the north door and walk into Room B1-14. Open the chest. (If the blue wall is blocking the chest, go a room with a Crystal Switch, hit it, then return to this room.)

The Map

Immediately after opening the Big Chest in Room B1-18, walk west into Room B1-17 and open the chest. (You can also enter this room from Room B1-13.)

The Big Chest (Cane of Somaria)

Enter Room B1-18 through the southwest door. Use the Hookshot to swing across the room, then run up the walkway as it collapses behind you. At the north end of the room, open the Big Chest.

Beating the Boss (Vitreous)

Stand on one side of the room and smack away the eyeballs with your Sword. Keep destroying

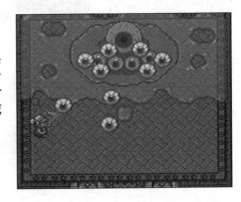

the eyeballs until there are only four left and Vitreous pulls itself out of the slime to attack you. Hit Vitreous with the Spin Attack.

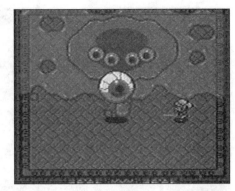

Room B2-4: Button Pushing

Use the Cane of Somaria to create a Somarian block and push it onto the button.

TURTLE ROCK (D-H1/C)

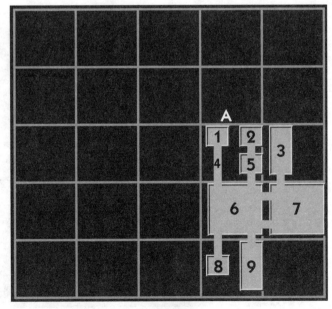

Floor 1F

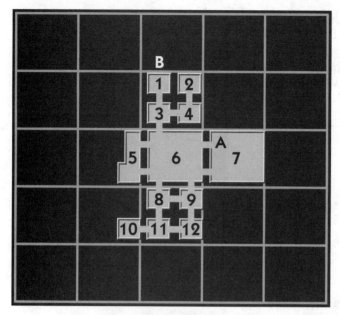

Floor B1

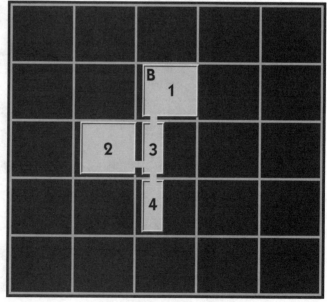

Floor B2

Floor B3

Getting Inside

Go to L-A8/C and walk onto the plateau with three wooden stakes. Use the Magic Hammer to smash the lower-right stake, then the upper stake, then the lower-left stake, to make a Warp Tile appear. Walk onto the

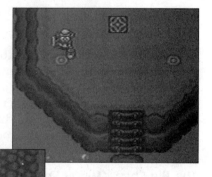

tile to appear on top of Turtle Rock. Walk onto the Quake Medallion symbol and use the Quake Medallion to open the door into Turtle Rock.

The Big Key

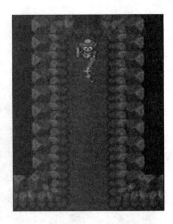

Go to the northwest corner of Room B1-6 and enter the tube on the right. You'll slide into the northwest corner of the room. Walk west into Room B1-5 and kill the bouncing creature for a Key. Open the south door and walk into Room B1-6. Enter the tube and you'll slide to the chest in the middle of the room. Open the chest.

The Compass

Go to Room 1F-8 and open the chest, then face south and hold down the B button to charge for a Spin Attack. Don't release the button; keep holding it down as you walk through the north door. This is the only way to get out of this room.

The Map

Go to Room 1F-7 and create a floating platform. Walk onto the platform and push Down to start it moving. Make the Fire Rod your active item. Wait until the platform is below the lower-left torch in the cluster of four torches, then light all of the torches with the Rod. When the platform comes to a stop, run through the north door into Room 1F-3. Open the left chest at the north end of the room.

The Big Chest (Mirror Shield)

Go to Room B1-10 and bomb through the south wall. Go outside and walk to the eastern entrance. (This is the time to collect Container Piece 24; see Chapter 4 for more details.) Go into the eastern entrance and you'll be in Room B1-12. Use the Cane of Somaria to cross the gap and open the Big Chest.

Beating The Boss (Trinexx)

Shoot Trinexx's
left head with the
Ice Rod and
destroy it with the
Sword. (Don't use
the Spin Attack,
just hack away.)
Shoot Trinexx's
right head with
the Fire Rod and
use Sword swings
to destroy it.
When both heads
have been de-

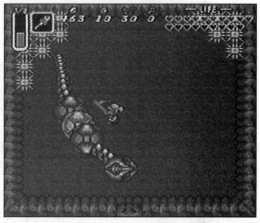

stroyed, Trinexx turns into a long snakelike creature. Hit
Trinexx in the midsection with the Spin Attack.

Room 1F-1: Chain Chomps

Hit the Crystal Switch to lower the blue walls, then push the
block in the lower-left corner to make a hidden chest appear.
Hit the Crystal Switch again to lower the orange walls and
open the chest for a Key.

Room 1F-8: Question Mark?

Use the Came of Somaria on the question mark to create a floating platform. You'll be doing this throughout Turtle Rock, so bring plenty of Potions to restore your Magic Power.

Room B2-1:
Where's the Button?

Steer the floating platform into the middle of the room to find a button underneath a skull. Push the button to open the door into Room B2-3.

GANON'S TOWER (D-E1/C)

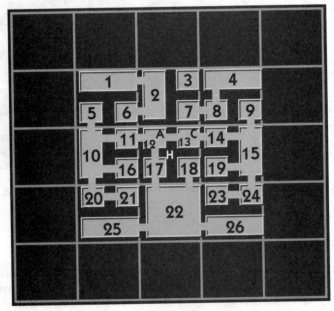

Floor 1F

Floor 2F

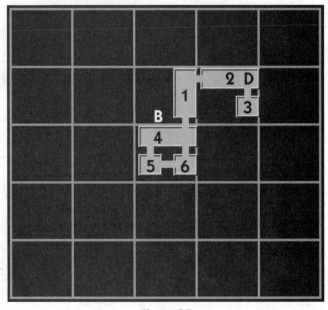

Floor 3F

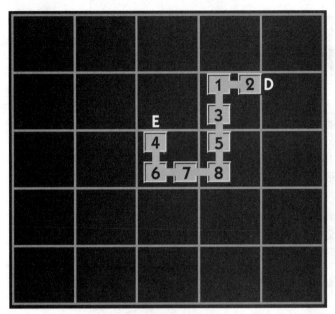

Floor 4F

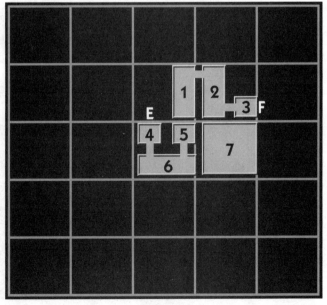

Floor 5F

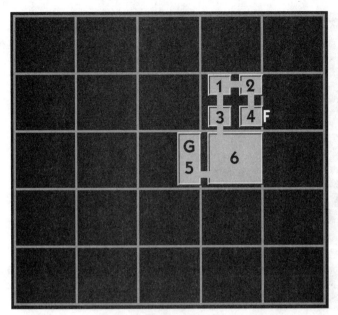

Floor 6F

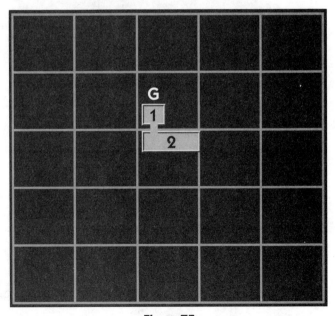

Floor 7F

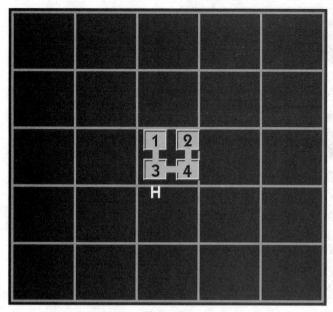

Floor B1

Getting Inside

Walk to the front of the Tower and the Crystals in your possession will combine their magical powers to create an entrance.

The Big Key

Go to Room 1F-22 and light the torch to light up the hidden walkways. Run across the pathways and enter Room B1-18. Bomb through the crack in the southeast corner of the room and drop into Room B1-4. Defeat the Armos Knights and go north into Room B1-2. Open the middle chest for the Big Key.

The Compass

Open the northwest chest in Room 1F-23.

The Map

Go to Room 1F-16 and open the chest.

The Big Chest (Red Mail)

Immediately after collecting, go to Room B1-3 and climb up the stairs to Room 1F-17. Open the Big Chest.

Beating the Boss (Agahnim)

In your second battle, Agahnim attacks with two "clones" of himself. The fake Agahnims are easy to spot, since they're hazy and transparent. Use the Sword or Bug-Catching Net to deflect Agahnim's  energy balls back at him. Agahnim doesn't attack with lightning this time, so don't worry about having to dodge that particular attack.

Room 1F-4: Hard To Cross

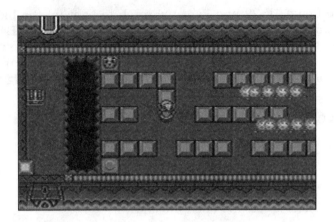

Walk to the west side of the room and push the single block to make a hidden chest appear. Latch onto the chest with the Hookshot to swing across the gap, then open the chest for a Key.

Room 1F-15: Light My Fire

Light the four torches to open the south door into Room 1F-24.

Room 1F-22: Relight My Fire

Walk to the northwest corner of the room, then walk to the right until you see the torch. Use the Fire Rod to light the torch and light up the invisible walkways. The torch only stays lit for a brief period of time, so if it goes out while you're still on the walkways, use the Ether Medallion.

Room 1F-24: Conveyor Belt

Create a Somarian Block, pick it up and throw it onto the conveyor belt, then press the Y button to make it explode and hit the Switch.

Room B1-4: Return of the Armos Knights

Stand in a corner and shoot the Knights with your Bow. It takes three Arrows to destroy each Knight. If you run out of Arrows, use your Sword. When you've destroyed all but one of the Knights, the final Knight starts moving around rapidly. Keep moving and remember that you can hit the last Knight whether he's on the ground or in the air.

Room 3F-3: Dash Bounce

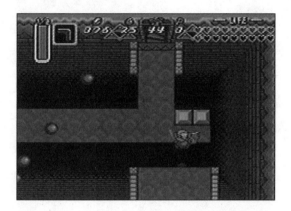

Walk to the eastern side of the room and stand underneath the two blocks. Start a Dash Attack, then turn toward the blocks just before you start Dashing. you'll bounce off the blocks and across to the ledge. Bomb through the wall and go into Room 3F-3 to find two Small Faeries.

Room 4F-6: Return of the Lanmolas

Whenever a Lanmola bursts out of the ground, stand above, below, or to either side to avoid the rocks caused by the bursting. Use the Spin Attack to hit the Lanmolas in the head. You can also use your Bow, but the Spin Attack does far more damage. The last Lanmola kicks out rocks in eight directions, making it harder to dodge them.

Room 6F-6: Return of the Moldorm

Use the Spin Attack to hit the Moldorm in the tail. If you fall off the platform, or through the hole in the middle of the platform, you'll have to climb back up and once again battle the Moldorm—and it regains all of its energy when you fall.

After you defeat the Moldorm, walk south and you'll see a chest. Latch onto the chest with the Hookshot and swing across.

Faeries

INTRODUCTION

Faeries are flying creatures who recharge your Heart
Containers with their healing magic. Faeries also live in the
Mysterious Ponds, which have strange effects of their own.
There are two types of Faeries: Large Faeries, which heal all of
your Containers, and Small Faeries, with lesser healing
powers. We've listed the locations of all Faeries in the Light
and Dark Worlds below (excluding the locations of Faeries in
Death Mountain).

By the way, when you encounter a Large Faerie, you'll see the only typo in the game. The Large Faerie says "I will **sooth** your wounds..." when she should say "I will **soothe** your wounds..." Just thought you'd wanna know.

LIGHT WORLD LARGE FAERIES

Near the Middle-Aged Man (C7/S)

Enter the cave west of the Middle-Aged Man to find a Large Faerie.

Near Link's House (E7/NE)

Walk south of Link's House, then walk into the northeast corner of the Great Swamp. Bomb through the rocks to reveal a cave entrance. Enter the cave to find a Large Faerie.

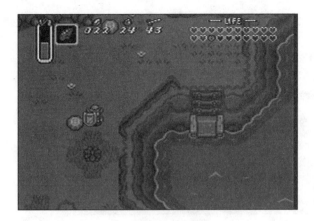

Near the Graveyard (F3/NW)

Look for a small patch of grass and chop down the bush in the middle of the patch to reveal a hidden hole. Drop into the hole to find a Large Faerie.

Near the Eastern Palace (G5/S)

Look for a cave entrance above the row of five trees. Enter the cave to find a Large Faerie.

LIGHT WORLD SMALL FAERIES

Near the Lumberjacks' House (C1/C)

Use the Dash Attack to smash into the strangely colored tree that the Lumberjack Twins were cutting down earlier. The top of the tree bursts apart when you Dash into it, revealing a secret entrance in the trunk. Drop into the trunk, climb up the stairs, and walk north to find four Small Faeries.

Near Link's House (D5/SE)

Walk northwest of Link's House and look for a rock pile. Dash Attack the rock pile to reveal hidden stairs. Go down the stairs to find four Small Faeries.

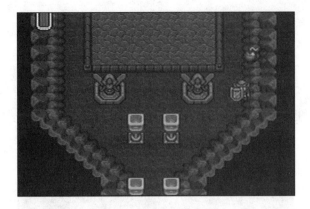

The Fountain of Happiness (G7/C)

Bomb through the wall to the right of the Fountain. Walk through the wall to find four Small Faeries.

Near the Eastern Palace (H6/NE)

Look for a cave entrance near a group of stakes. Enter the cave and follow the corridor to find four Small Faeries. (If you have the Flute, fly to Location 5 and you'll be dropped off just west of the cave.)

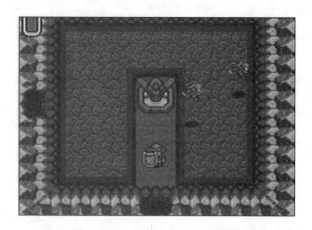

Near Lake Hylia (H6/SW)

Enter the cave northeast of Lake Hylia. Bomb through the north wall. Walk through the wall to find two Small Faeries. (You can also collect the Good Bee at this location.)

DARK WORLD LARGE FAERIES

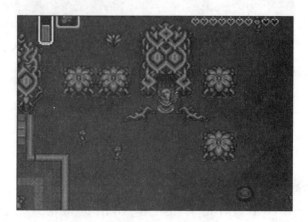

East Misery Maze Entrance (B6/SW)

There are three "mouth" entrances to the Misery Maze Dungeon. Go into the east entrance to find a Large Faerie.

Near the Dark Palace (G5/S)

Look for a cave entrance above the row of five trees. Enter the cave to find a Large Faerie. (This is in the same place as a Large Faerie in the Light World.)

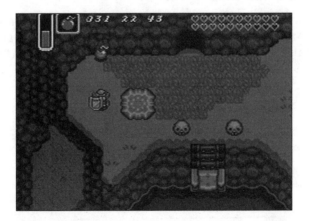

Near Lake Hylia (H6/SW)

Walk to the cave northeast of Lake Hylia. Bomb through the crack to the left of the cave to reveal a hidden cave entrance. Walk through the crack to find a Large Faerie. (This is in the same place as the Ice Rod in the Light World.)

DARK WORLD SMALL FAERIES

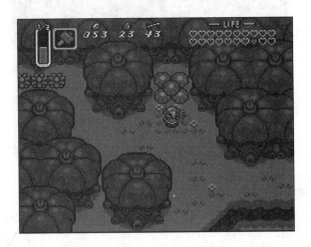

Near the Bomb Shop (D5/SE)

Walk northwest of the Bomb Shop and look for a rock pile. Dash Attack the rock pile to reveal hidden stairs. Go down the stairs to find four Small Faeries. (This is in the same place as four Faeries in the Light World.)

Heart Containers

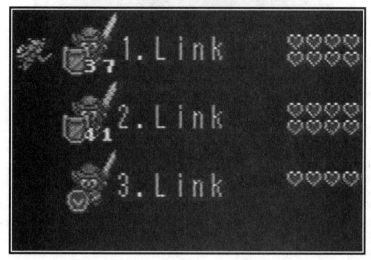

INTRODUCTION

At the start of the game, you have only three Heart
Containers; by the end of the game, you can have twenty
Containers. Eleven of the Containers are earned when you
defeat Dungeon Bosses. The other six Containers are divided
up into twenty-four Heart Container Pieces (we'll just call
them Pieces from here on) and scattered around the Light and
Dark Worlds.

In this chapter, we'll tell you where every Piece is and how to get it. Keep in mind that you won't be able to get some Pieces without first collecting a certain Item or completing a certain task.

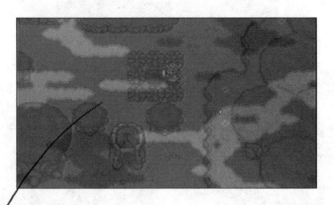

Piece 1 (Lost Woods)

Walk to the Fortune Teller's hut at L-B3/N and go north into the Lost Woods. Keep going north until you find a 3-by-3 cluster of bushes. Chop down the middle bush and fall into the hole. You'll land right next to the Piece.

Piece 2 (Thieves' Hideout)

Enter the Thieves' Hideout at L-B4/N and go down to Floor B1. Bomb through the crack in the north wall. Walk through the wall and open the chest for the Piece.

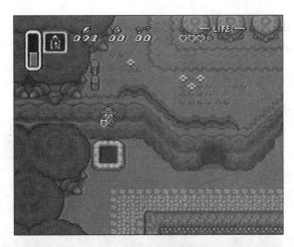

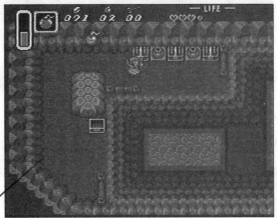

Piece 3 (Kakariko Village)

Walk to the well at L-A4/NE. Jump into the well from the ledge above. When you land, Bomb through the crack in the north wall. Walk through the wall and open the chest for the Piece.

Piece 4 (House of the Quarreling Brothers)

Enter the House of the Quarreling Brothers at L-B6/C. Bomb through the wall in the middle of the House (if you haven't done so already) and the Brothers become best buds again. Walk out the left side of the House and talk to the woman, then play the 15-Second Game.

Winning the Game is a cinch-o-rama with the picture we've provided here. Talk to the man at the end of the racecourse to receive the Piece.

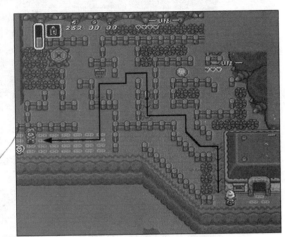

Piece 5 (Watergate)

Enter the Watergate at L-D8/E and walk north to the levers. Pull the lever on the right to open the dam and drain the water in the Great Swamp. Walk outside and you'll see the Piece just left of the Watergate.

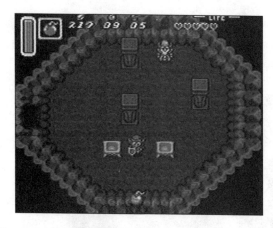

Piece 6 (Desert of Mystery)

Enter the cave at L-B7/NE, in the northeast corner of the Desert of Mystery. Talk to Aginah the Wise Man, then Bomb through the south wall in Aginah's room. Walk through the wall and open the chest for the Piece.

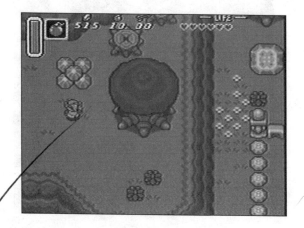

Piece 7 (Near the Sanctuary)

Walk west of the Sanctuary and look for a pile of rocks next to a large tree. Ram into the rocks with the Dash Attack. Climb down the stairs and open the chest for the Piece.

Piece 8 (Desert of Mystery)

Enter the Desert Palace at L-A7/NE and leave via the west exit. Walk south to find the Piece next to a hungry vulture.

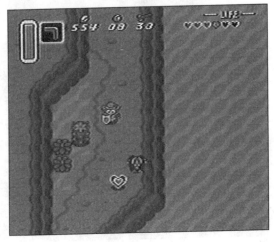

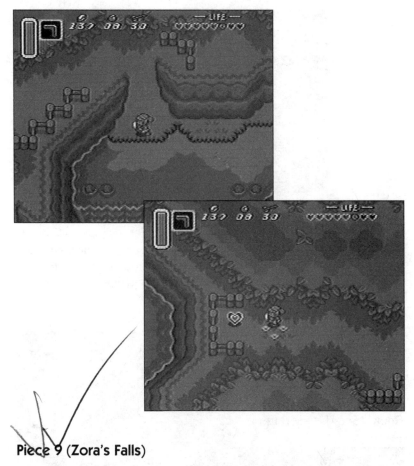

Piece 9 (Zora's Falls)

Walk to Zora's Falls at L-H2/N. If you already have the Flippers, go to where you bought them from Zora. If you don't have the Flippers yet, bring 500 Rupees with you and buy them from Zora. Swim south of Zora's Falls and go over the waterfall, then walk west. Don't go over the second waterfall or you'll have to swim back here. Walk up the grassy slope and move west to find the Piece.

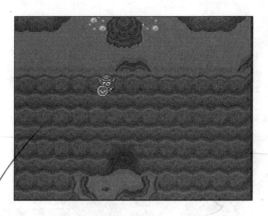

Piece 10 (Death Mountain)

Walk to Spectacle Rock at L-E1/SW. There's a rock formation in front of the Rock. Stand on the left side of the formation and jump down to the ledge below. Enter the cave and climb up to Floor 2F to find the Piece.

Piece 11 (Spectacle Rock)

In the Dark World, use the Magic Mirror to appear on Spectacle Rock. (See the section on

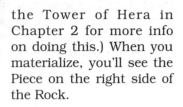

the Tower of Hera in Chapter 2 for more info on doing this.) When you materialize, you'll see the Piece on the right side of the Rock.

Piece 12 (Lumberjacks' House)

You can't collect this Piece until you've defeated Agahnim in Hyrule Castle. Walk to L-C1/C and use the Dash Attack to smash into the strangely colored tree that the Lumberjack Twins were cutting down earlier. The top of the tree bursts apart when you Dash into it, revealing a secret entrance in the trunk. Drop into the trunk, climb up the stairs, and Bomb through the east wall. Walk through the wall and collect the Piece.

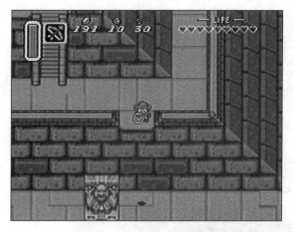

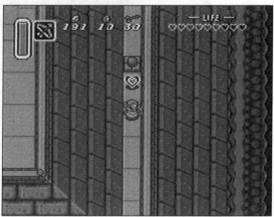

Piece 13 (Pyramid of Power)

Climb to the top of the Pyramid at D-E3/SW. Walk down the first flight of stairs, then walk down the flight of stairs on the right. Walk to the right and leap off the ledge down to the next lever. Walk east and north to find the Piece.

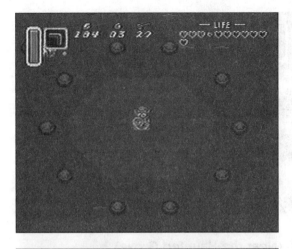

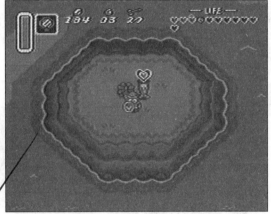

Piece 14 (Lake Hylia)

Swim to D-F7/E and locate a circle of stones. Walk into the middle of the circle and use the Magic Mirror. You'll appear on a small island with the Piece on the ground.

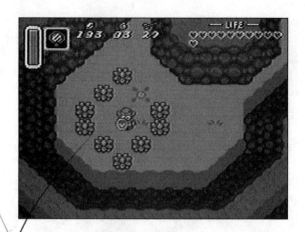

Piece 15 (Near the Haunted Grove)

Walk to D-C7/SW and locate a circle of bushes. Walk into the middle of the circle and use the Magic Mirror. You'll appear on a plateau. Enter the cave and collect the Piece.

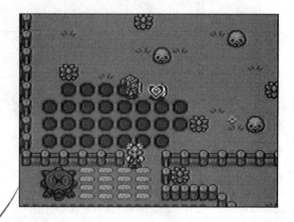

Piece 16 (Treasure Field)

Walk to D-A6/NE and pay the gatekeeper 80 Rupees to dig in the Treasure Field. Keep playing (and digging) until you find the Piece.

Piece 17 (Near the Cemetery)

Walk onto the small ledge at D-E3/N, just north of the
Cemetery. Use the Magic Mirror, enter the cave, and Bomb
through the east wall. Walk through the hole and collect the
Piece.

Piece 18 (Near Death Mountain)

Walk to D-C2/NE and read the sign: "I'll give a Piece of Heart
to the person who wears the Cape." Walk east, yank up the
rock, and enter the cave. Go north and climb to Floor 2F. Use

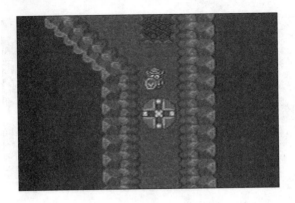

the Hookshot to cross the hole in the floor, then put on the Magic Cape to walk past the Bumper. Walk outside and collect the Piece.

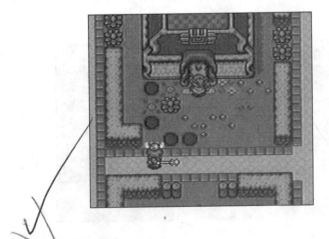

Piece 19 (Chest Game)

Enter the hut at D-A4/E in the Village of Outcasts. Pay the storekeeper 30 Rupees to play the Chest Game. Keep playing until you find the Piece.

Piece 20 (Near the Blacksmith's House)

Walk to the field of stakes just south of the Blacksmith's House at D-C4/S. Use the Magic Hammer to smash all of the stakes into the ground. When you hit the last stake, some secret stairs appear just south of the stakes. Go down the stairs and collect the Piece.

Piece 21 (Near the Misery Maze)

Use the Flute in the Light World and fly to Location 6. When you land, pick up the rock on the right and walk onto the Warp Tile. Walk north to the Misery Maze Dungeon and go into the west entrance at D-A6/SE. Go down the stairs and open the left chest to collect the Piece.

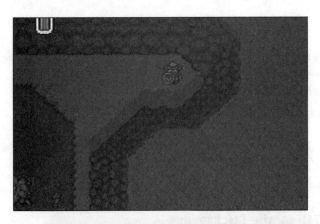

Piece 22 (Misery Mire)

Walk to D-B6/S, which is the extreme northeast corner of the Misery Mire. Use the Magic Mirror and pick up the stone to reveal a hidden cave. Enter the cave and push through the blocks to collect the Piece.

Piece 23 (Death Mountain)

Walk to D-G1/E (one screen west of Turtle Rock) and look for a large stone. Pick up the stone to reveal a hidden cave. Enter the cave and walk north. Use the Cane of Somaria, or the Ether Medallion, to cross the invisible bridge. Once you've crossed the bridge, Bomb through the wall. Walk through the wall into the next room and Bomb through the west wall. (Bomb through the north wall to find a Faerie.) Walk west and south to go outside. Use the Magic Mirror and collect the Piece.

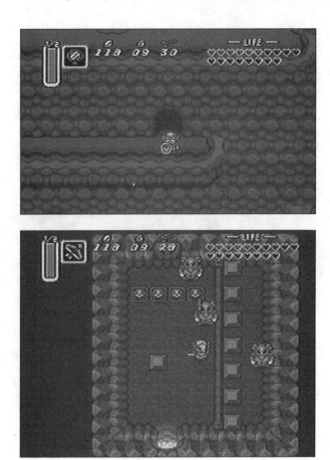

Piece 24 (Death Mountain)

Enter the Turtle Rock Dungeon (D-H1/C) and walk down to
Floor B1. Use either exit to walk outside onto the narrow
ledge. Move directly in front of the door on the right and use
the Magic Mirror. Enter the cave and kill the green Goriyas
and open the door. Smash the Moles with the Magic Hammer
and walk through the door to collect the Piece.

5

Items

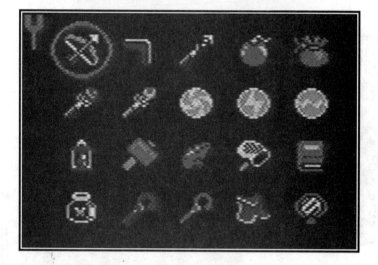

INTRODUCTION

This Chapter is an alphabetically arranged list of all the items and weapons to be found in LTP. Each item or weapon (usually) has three bits of information: Location (where to get it), How Obtained (how to get it), and Function (what to do with it).

Seven types of items are listed in groups: Boomerangs, Canes, Clothes, Gloves, Medallions, Shields, and Swords. For example, both the Cane of Bryna and the Cane of Somaria are found under Canes.

BOMB

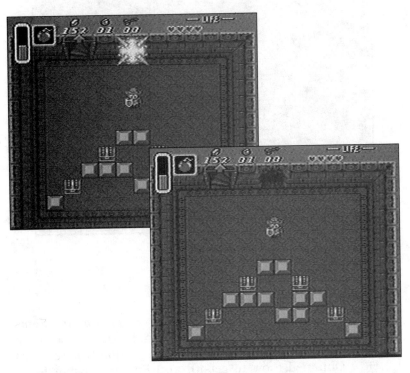

Location: Shops and chests throughout the Light and Dark Worlds.

How Obtained: Buy them at shops or find them in chests.

Function: Bombs blow holes in floors and walls. Most hidden rooms in the Dungeons are found by using a Bomb to blow through a wall. After you drop a Bomb, you can pick it up and throw it with the A button.

At the start of LTP, you can carry up to ten Bombs. This capacity can be increased at the Pond of Happiness. (See the Pond of Happiness in Chapter 6.)

BOOK OF MUDORA

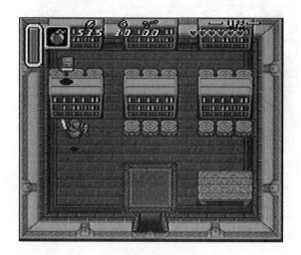

Location: House of Books (L-B5/S).

How Obtained: Use a Dash Attack to run into the bookshelf. The Book of Mudora drops to the floor so you can pick it up.

Function: The Book of Mudora is your translation guide to Mudoran, the written language of Hyrule. (Actually, only a few signs are written in Mudoran; most of them are written in plain English. And why is it "Mudoran?" Shouldn't it be "Hyrulian?") Two of the three Medallions can't be obtained without the Book, and you also need it to enter the Desert Palace Dungeon.

BOOMERANGS

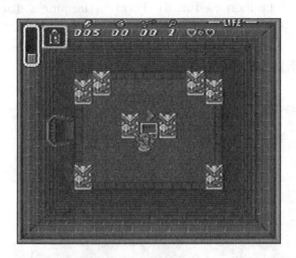

Blue Boomerang

Location: Hyrule Castle (L-E4/NW).

How Obtained: Go to Room B1-4 and open the chest.

Red Boomerang

Location: Waterfall of Wishing (L-H2/NW).

How Obtained: Throw the Blue Boomerang into the Mysterious Pond. When the Faerie appears, tell her the truth and she'll turn the Blue Boomerang into the Red Boomerang before giving it back to you.

Function: The Boomerang has two uses. Throw it at your enemies to stun them for a few seconds. Throw it at distant objects to pick them up. The Red Boomerang has a longer range than the Blue Boomerang.

BOW AND ARROWS

Bow

Location: The Big Chest of the Eastern Palace (L-H3/S).

Arrows

Location: Shops, chests, and Dungeons throughout the Light and Dark Worlds.

How Obtained: Buy them at shops, find them in chests, or kill enemies that use Arrows to attack and they may drop some.

Silver Arrows

Location: Fat Faerie inside the Pyramid of Power (D-D4/E).

How Obtained: Throw the Bow into the Mysterious Pond. When the Fat Faerie appears, tell her the truth and she'll turn your Arrows into Silver Arrows before giving the Bow back to you.

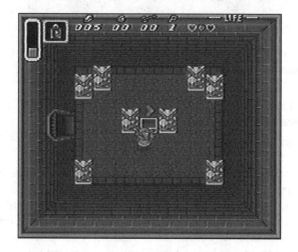

Function: The Bow is a powerful weapon that you'll need to defeat several Bosses (including the mighty Ganon). It uses Arrows for ammo. At the start of LTP, you can carry up to thirty Arrows. This number can be increased at the Pond of Happiness. (See the Pond of Happiness in Chapter 6.) To defeat Ganon, you need Silver Arrows from the Fat Faerie. (See the Fat Faerie in Chapter 6.)

BUG-CATCHING NET

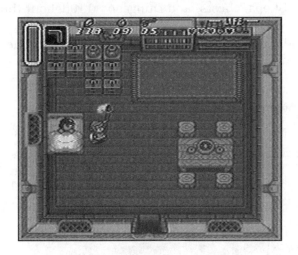

Location: Bug-Catching Kid's House in Kakariko Village (L-B4/S).

How Obtained: Visit the Kid with at least one Magic Bottle in your possession and he'll give you the Net.

Function: The Bug-Catching Net catches Faeries and Bees so you can throw 'em into Magic Bottles for later use. If you die with a Bottled Faerie in your inventory, the Faerie resurrects you and you'll continue playing. Bottled Bees can be unleashed on your enemies to attack them and cause damage. There's one extra-special Bee called the Good Bee. (See the Ice Cave in Chapter 6.) Finally, you can use the Net in battle against Agahnim to deflect his energy balls (although the Sword also does this).

CANES

Cane of Byrna

Location: Atop Death Mountain (L-E1/S).

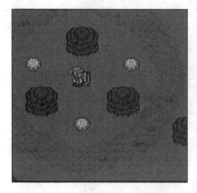
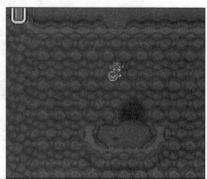

How Obtained: Use the Warp Tile at the above location to enter the Dark World. Walk south to the edge of the cliff and jump down to the ledge. Enter the cave and smash the Moles with the Magic Hammer. Run across the path of spikes (use the Magic Cape to avoid taking damage) until you reach the huge block. Pick up the block (you need the Titan's Mitt) and open the chest to collect the Cane.

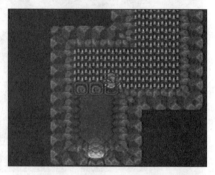

Function: The Cane of Byrna creates a magical shield that prevents you from taking damage. It sucks up Magic Power like crazy, so use it sparingly.

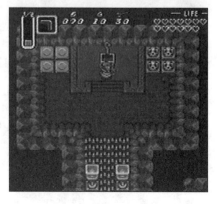

Cane of Somaria

Location: The Big Chest of the Misery Maze (D-A7/NW).

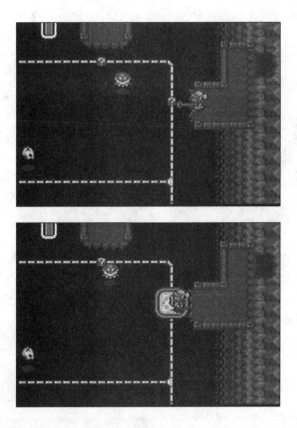

Function: The Cane of Somaria creates Somarian blocks, which serve multiple purposes. Press the Y button to create a Somarian block. Now you can do three things with the block: push it, pick it up and throw it, or make it explode in four directions by pressing the Y button again. The Cane of Somaria also creates floating platforms in the Turtle Rock Dungeon.

CLOTHING

Green Jerkin

Location: On your body when you start the adventure.

Blue Mail

Location: The Big Chest of Ice Island (D-G7/C).

Red Mail

Location: The Big Chest of Ganon's Tower (D-E1/C).

Function: The Green Jerkin that you start the game with actually doesn't absorb any damage at all. The Blue Mail absorbs about 25 percent of the damage you take. The Red Mail absorbs about 50 percent of the damage you take.

FIRE ROD

Location: The Big Chest of the Skull Palace.

Function: The Fire Rod lights torches and is an effective weapon against certain enemies and Bosses.

FLUTE

Location: In the upper-left corner of the Haunted Grove (L-C6/NE).

How Obtained: Get the Shovel (see below) and use the Magic Mirror to warp into the Light World. Dig around with the Shovel until you find

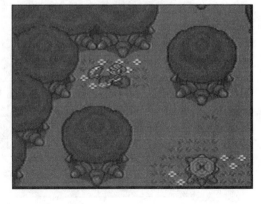

the Flute. Return to the Dark World and talk to the creature. He'll let you have the Flute if you play him a song. When you play the song, he turns into a tree. No, seriously.

Use the Magic Mirror to enter the Light World and walk to the Weathercock in the middle of Kakariko Village. Play the Flute and the Weathercock transforms into a magic Duck. Not exactly the most majestic of flying creatures, but he does the job.

From now on, when you play the Flute in the Light World, the Duck flies onto the

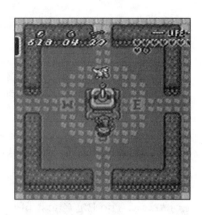

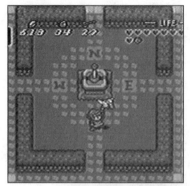

screen, grabs you, and takes you to one of eight locations. You can dodge the Duck by walking up or down when it flies onto the screen. You can't call the Duck when you're indoors; you have to be outside for it to hear you.

GLOVES

Power Glove

Location: The Big Chest of the Desert Palace (L-A7/NE).

Titan's Mitt

Location: The Big Chest of the Gargoyle's Domain (D-B4/C).

Function: The Power Glove (no relation to Mattel's virtual-reality NES controller) and the Titan's Mitt give you super strength to lift heavy rocks out of your way. The darker (and larger) a rock, the heavier it is. The Power Glove allows you to lift only light rocks, while the Titan's Mitt gives you strength to lift any and every rock.

HOOKSHOT

Location: The Big Chest of the Swamp Palace (D-D8/E).

Function: The Hookshot works two ways: as a grappling hook to swing across gaps, and as a Boomerang to stun enemies and pick up items.

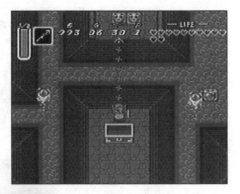

ICE ROD

Location: A hidden cave east of Lake Hylia.

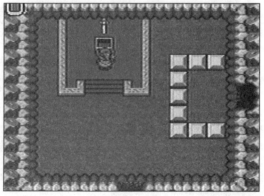

How Obtained: Walk to L-H6/SW to find a cave entrance. Bomb through the crack to the left of the cave, go through, and walk north to find the chest. Open the chest to collect the Ice Rod.

Function: The Ice Rod freezes some of your enemies solid. You can pick up frozen enemies and throw them. The Ice Rod is also used against one of the Bosses.

LAMP

Location: Link's House (L-E6/N) and several chests inside Hyrule Castle (L-E4/NW).

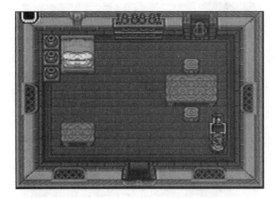

How Obtained: When your Uncle leaves the house, jump out of bed and open the chest in the southeast corner of the House to collect the Lamp. If you don't get the Lamp at this point, you'll find it in several of the chests in Hyrule Castle. (If you get the Lamp in the House, the chests will be filled with other items.)

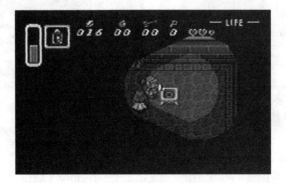

Function: The Lamp lights up dark Dungeons and allows you to light up torches (the gray square thingmabobs).

MAGIC BOTTLES

Magic Bottle 1

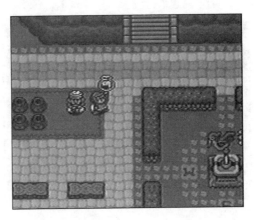

Location: The Merchant (L-B4/W, north of the Weathercock).
How Obtained: Buy the Bottle for 100 Rupees.

Magic Bottle 2

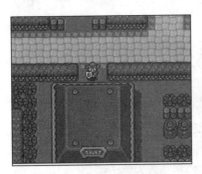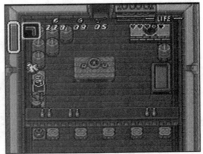

Location: The Inn (L-B4/S).
How Obtained: Walk through the north door of the Inn. Open the chest in the southwest corner of the room to collect the Bottle.

Magic Bottle 3

Location: Under the bridge at L-F6/N.

How Obtained: Jump into the water at L-F6/S, then swim north and underneath the bridge. Talk to the hobo and he'll give you his Bottle.

Magic Bottle 4

Location: The Dark World Blacksmith's House (D-C4/SE).

How Obtained: After reuniting the dwarf brothers at the Light World Blacksmith's House (L-C4/SE), go to the Dark World Blacksmith's House and you'll find a chest. Touch the chest and you'll start dragging it around behind you. Use the Magic Mirror to enter the Light World and walk to the Middle-Aged Man at L-C8/NE. Talk to him and he'll open the chest, giving you the Bottle inside.

Function: Magic Bottles hold Magic Potions, Faeries, and Bees. You can collect the first three Bottles near the start of the adventure, but you won't be able to get the fourth Bottle until much later on.

MAGIC CAPE

Location: The Graveyard (L-E3/N).

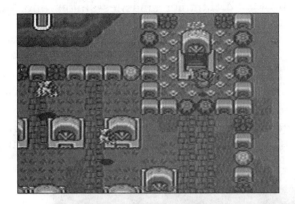

How Obtained: Dash Attack the easternmost tombstone in the Graveyard to reveal hidden stairs. Climb down the stairs and walk north to find the chest. Open the chest to collect the Magic Cape.

Function: The Magic Cape makes you invisible, and invulnerable to damage, but it's a real Magic Power hog. You need the Cape to collect one of the Heart Container Pieces.

MAGIC HAMMER

Location: The Big Chest of the Dark Palace (D-H3/S).

Function: The Magic Hammer smashes stakes and Moles into the ground.

MAGIC MIRROR

Location: In the possession of the Lost Old Man on Death Mountain.

How Obtained: Escort the Lost Old Man through the caves, to his hideout on Death Mountain, and he'll give you the Magic Mirror as a reward.

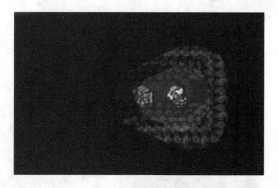

Function: The Magic Mirror transports you from the Dark World to the Light World, creating a "warp" at the point where you used the Mirror. If you touch the warp, you'll return to the Dark World. You need the Moon Pearl to retain your normal form in the Dark World (see below).

MAGIC MUSHROOM

Location: The Lost Woods (L-B1/S).

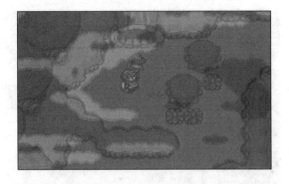

Heh heh. Thank you, young
man. Come back to the shop
later for something good.

How Obtained: Walk into it and you'll automatically take it.

Function: Take the Mushroom to the Witch's House (L-G3/C) and give it to her. Come back later and go into the House to collect a bag of Magic Powder as your reward.

MAGIC POWDER

Location: The Witch's House (L-G3/C).

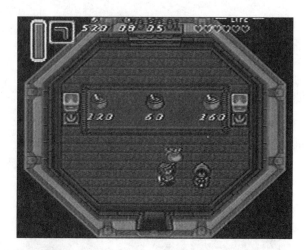

How Obtained: Bring the Witch the Magic Mushroom and return to the House later to pick up the bag of Powder.

Function: The Magic Powder has an unusual effect on two of your enemies, and is also used at the Smithy's Well to reduce your Magic Power usage by half.

The Buzzblob turns into . . .

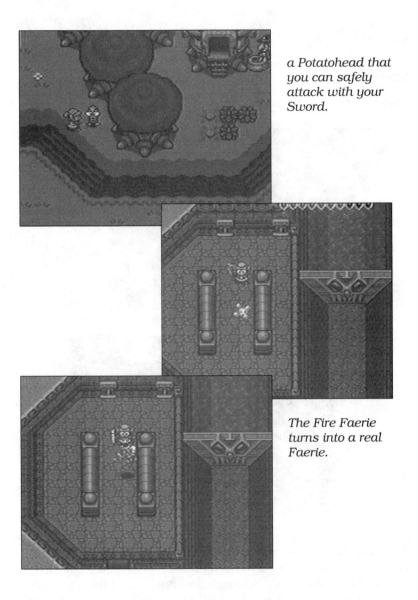

a Potatohead that
you can safely
attack with your
Sword.

The Fire Faerie
turns into a real
Faerie.

MEDALLIONS

Bombos Medallion

Location: D-C8/E.

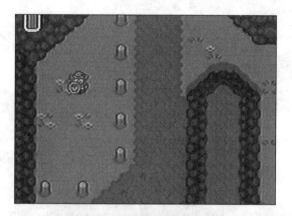

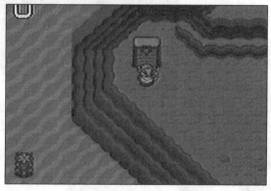

How Obtained: Stand inside the group of stakes at the location above and use the Magic Mirror to enter the Light World. Walk west to the Mudoran monolith and use the Book of Mudora to read the Monolith and collect the Bombos Medallion.

Function: The Bombos Medallion causes a big blast around Link, destroying all the enemies on the screen (except for Bosses).

Ether Medallion

Location: West of the Tower of Hera (L-E1/C).

How Obtained: Walk across the bridge west of the Tower of Hera to the Mudoran mono- lith. Use the Book of Mudora to read the monolith and collect the Ether Medallion.

Function: The Ether Medallion is needed to enter the Misery Mire Dungeon. It can also be used to light up invisible bridges for a few moments.

Quake Medallion

Location: The circle of stones in the Lake of Ill Omen (D-H2/N).

 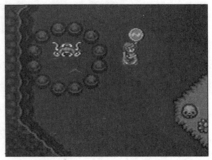

How Obtained: Pull up the sign on the shore, walk into the water, and throw the sign into the circle. A monster comes out of the water and gives you the Quake Medallion.

Function: The Quake Medallion is needed to enter the Turtle Rock Dungeon.

MOON PEARL

Location: The Big Chest in the Tower of Hera (L-E1/C).

Function: The Moon Pearl allows you to retain your normal form in the Dark World. Without the Pearl, when you enter the Dark World, you are humiliatingly turned into a pink bunny rabbit that can't attack, defend, or pick up items.

PEGASUS SHOES

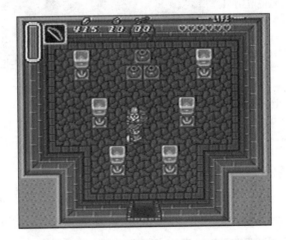

Location: Sahasralah's Hideout (L-G4/N).

How Obtained: Bring the Pendant of Courage from the Eastern Palace to Sahasralah. He'll be so impressed with your heroism that he'll give you the Shoes.

Function: The Pegasus Shoes give you the powerful Dash Attack. Hold down the A button for one second and Link starts to Dash. The Dash Attack knocks items out of trees and smashes apart rock piles.

SHIELDS

Fighter's Shield

Location: With your injured Uncle in the tunnel beneath Hyrule Castle (L-E4/NW).

How Obtained: When you find your injured Uncle, he'll give you the Fighter's Shield.

Red Shield

Location: The Waterfall of Wishing (L-H2/NW) and the Item Shop (D-C4/NE).

How Obtained: At the Waterfall of Wishing, throw your Fighter's Shield into the Mysterious Pond. When the Faerie appears, tell her the truth and she'll turn the Fighter's Shield into the Red Shield before giving it back to you. At the Item Shop, buy it for 500 Rupees.

Mirror Shield

Location: The Big Chest of Turtle Rock (D-H1/C).

Function: The Shields deflect missile attacks. The most powerful Shield, the Mirror Shield, even deflects laser beams. There's one creature, the Pikit, that tries to swallow your Shield as you walk past. It can swallow the Fighter's Shield and the Red Shield, but it can't nab the Mirror Shield.

SHOVEL

Location: In the possession of the creature at D-C6/NE.

How Obtained: Talk to the creature and agree to look for his Flute. He'll give you the Shovel.

Function: Use the Shovel to dig around the Haunted Grove (L-C6/NE) and find the Flute.

SWORDS

Fighter's Sword

Location: With your injured Uncle in the tunnel beneath Hyrule Castle (L-E4/NW).

How Obtained: When you find your injured Uncle, he'll give you the Fighter's Sword.

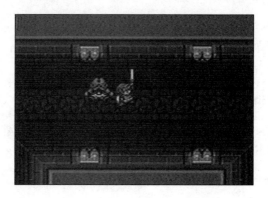

Master Sword

Location: The northwest corner of the Lost Woods (L-A1/C).

How Obtained: After obtaining the three Pendants, walk to the above location and the Pendants' magic will automatically free the Sword.

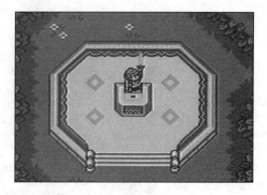

Tempered Sword

Location: The Blacksmith's House (L-C4/SE).

How Obtained: Walk to D-B5/S and you'll find a frog trapped behind some heavy rocks. Pick up the rocks and talk to the frog, then take him to the Light World Smithy. (When you use the Mirror, he'll turn from a frog into a dwarf.) Enter the Smithy and the Brothers will be reunited.

Go outside, come back in, and the Brothers will offer to temper your Sword for ten Rupees. Pay the amount, go wander around for a while, then come back and take the Sword.

Golden Sword

Location: The Fat Faerie in the Pyramid of Power (D-D4/E).

How Obtained: Throw the Tempered Sword into the Mysterious Pond. When the Fat Faerie appears, tell her the truth and she'll turn the Tempered Sword into the Golden Sword before giving it back to you.

Function: The Sword is your main weapon throughout LTP. Hold down the B button to charge the Sword for a Spin Attack (a very useful maneuver against the Bosses). If you have the Master Sword (or a more powerful Sword), and your Heart Containers are full, the Sword shoots a powerful beam.

ZORA'S FLIPPERS

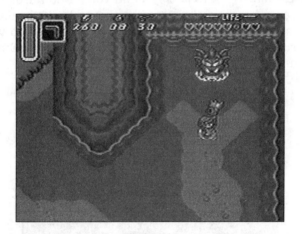

Location: Zora's Falls (L-H2/N).

How Obtained: Buy the Flippers from Zora for 500 Rupees.

Function: Zora's Flippers give you the ability to swim, which you need to reach many special items and locations. Buy the Flippers ASAP.

Locations

INTRODUCTION

No, this chapter doesn't give you every single location in LTP; that would be going just a teensy bit overboard. Instead, it lists important locations, places that you may want to (or have to) visit at least once during the course of your adventure.

The locations are divided into two sections, Light World and Dark World, and are in alphabetical order. Map coordinates are provided for every location.

LIGHT WORLD LOCATIONS

Blacksmith's House (C4/SE)

This House is just east of Kakariko Village. The Blacksmith can turn the Master Sword into a Tempered Sword, but he needs to find his missing partner first. The Blacksmith also has a mysterious Well in his front yard. Could it hide a secret? You know it!

Blacksmith's Well (C4/SE)

You need to fall into the Well from the ledge above, but you can't walk onto the ledge until you have the Magic Hammer. (A stake blocks the ledge.) Once you've fallen inside, walk

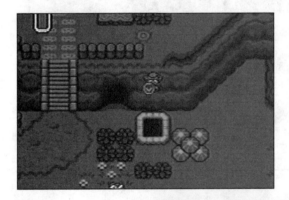

north and you'll find a strange altar. Sprinkle Magic Powder on the red jewel in the middle of the altar and a strange creature appears. He says that he's halved your Magic Power, but in fact, he's doubled it.

Bug-Catching Kid's House (B4/S)

The Kid's House is just north of the Inn. Come here with at least one Magic Bottle in your possession and talk to the Kid. He'll give you the Bug-Catching Net.

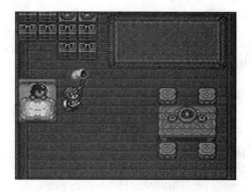

Den of Thieves (B2/NE)

There are two entrances to the Den, one obvious and one hidden. The obvious entrance is the tree stump. The hidden entrance is underneath the 3x3 bush cluster just above the tree stump. Inside the Den, you'll find a Container Piece and a thief who reveals a secret about the Middle-Aged Man in the Desert of Mystery.

Desert Palace (A7/NE)

The Power Glove and the second Pendant are located here.

Eastern Palace (H3/S)

The Bow and the first Pendant are located here.

Fortune Tellers (B3/NE, F6/SW)

The Fortune Tellers give you hints in exchange for Rupees. Of course, this book has all the hints of the Fortune Tellers, along with about a billion more of them. Do I really need to tell you not to spend your Rupees on them? Of course I don't.

Game of Chance (B1/NE)

This game seems like a good deal—pay 100 Rupees and keep whatever's inside the chest that you open—but it's not. Notice that the guy running it looks just like the guy in the Den of Thieves. Coincidence? Nuh-uh. Most of the time, you'll only find a single Rupee inside your chest. Avoid this "game" like the plague.

Game of Chance (B6/NW)

This game is completely legit, unlike the one in the Lost Woods. Pay 20 Rupees and open one of the three chests. You get to keep whatever's inside. However, even though you can win Rupees this way, there are much better ways of collecting them, namely, the Rupee Room and the Shooting Gallery. Don't waste your money here.

Graveyard (E3/N)

You can move the tombstones in the Graveyard, but most of them don't have anything underneath except restless ghosts. The two important stones are in the northwest corner and on the eastern side of the Graveyard.

The northwest stone leads into the passages below Hyrule Castle that lead to the Sanctuary. Remember those cracked walls you passed earlier but didn't have any Bombs to open? Well, now you can open 'em with a Bomb or with a Dash Attack. In the hidden chamber, you'll find Bombs, Arrows and 300 Rupees.

The easternmost stone leads into an underground chamber. Walk to the north end of the chamber and open the chest to find the Magic Cape.

Haunted Grove (C6/NE)

In the middle of the Grove, a ghostly boy plays his Flute for the peaceful forest critters of Hyrule. You can't talk to the boy and you can't catch the animals. They're just ghosts. Once you collect the Flute, the boy and the animals don't appear anymore.

House of Books (B5/S)

The most interesting reading material in this House is the Book of Mudora. You can't reach the Book, but you can knock it off the bookshelf if you Dash Attack into the shelf with the Pegasus Shoes.

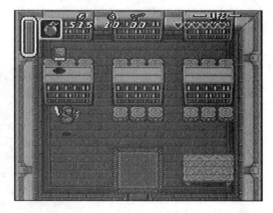

House of the Quarreling Brothers (B6/C)

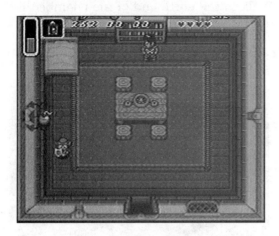

Blow up the wall in the middle of the House and the Brothers will apologize. More importantly, you'll now have access to the 15-Second Game. Walk out of the left door and talk to the woman to play. Win the game and you earn a Container Piece.

Hyrule Castle (E4/NW)

The home of Agahnim and the prison of Princess Zelda, the Castle has three separate dungeon levels (referred to in this book as "Rescuing Zelda," "Escaping to Sanctuary," and "Climbing to Agahnim").

Ice Cave (H6/SW)

Dash Attack the statue next to the Small Faeries and a magical Good Bee appears. Capture the Bee with the Net and put it in a Bottle. When you release the Bee, it attacks any

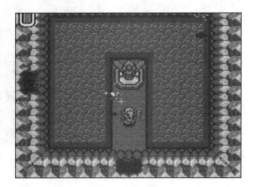

enemies within range, then flies back to you and hovers around, waiting for more enemies to appear. Recapture the Bee before you enter a new area, or it disappears, which means you'll have to get another one from the statue.

Inn (B4/S)

The Inn has two entrances. The south entrance is visible, but the north entrance can't be seen. Just walk through the space between the hedges and you'll go through the door. There's a Magic Bottle inside the chest in the north half of the Inn.

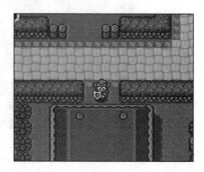

Item Shops (Numerous Locations)

Never, ever, EVER buy anything at an Item Shop. You can always get the items for lower prices (or even for free) at other locations: Bombs from the Mysterious Hut, Medicine from the Magic Shop, and so on and so forth.

Link's House (E6/N)

You start the adventure in this humble abode. The Lamp is inside the chest, and there are three Small Hearts underneath the jars in the northwest corner of the House. The Small Hearts reappear if you go outside and come back inside again.

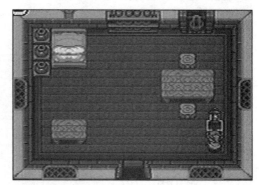

Magic Shop (G3/C)

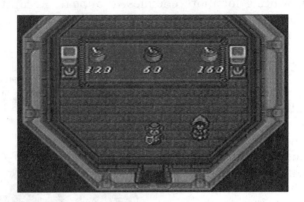

The Witch outside of the Shop needs a Magic Mushroom for her brew. Bring it to her from the Lost Woods, come back to the Shop later, and go inside to find your reward, a bag of Magic Powder.

Inside the Shop, you can buy all three types of Potions. Red Potion (120 Rupees) refills your Heart Containers. Green Potion (60 Rupees) refills your Magic Power. Blue Potion (160 Rupees) refills both your Heart Containers and your Magic Power. You shouldn't buy Green Potion, since you can get it for free at the Waterfall of Wishing, but the Blue Potion is an excellent investment. You should buy some Blue Potion before entering a new dungeon.

Merchant (B4/W)

The Merchant has a Magic Bottle on sale for 100 Rupees. The Merchant will also buy two "items" from you: the Good Bee (for 100 Rupees) and a Fish from the Great Swamp (for Rupees and other goodies).

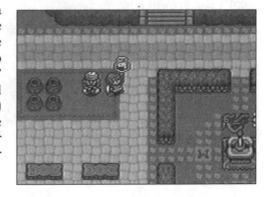

Middle-Aged Man (C8/NE)

You're looking at his gut, aren't ya?! He's workin' on it! And he'll also work on a chest that you'll find in the Dark World, opening it up and giving you the Magic Bottle inside.

Mysterious Hut (A5/C)

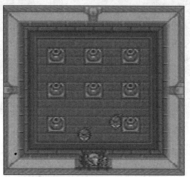

Plant a Bomb in front of the Hut and create a hole for you to walk inside. Kill the two rats inside the Hut and pick up the jars to find two Rupees, four Bombs, and five Arrows. If you leave the Hut and go back inside, the items regenerate, making this a handy place to go when you need Bombs and Arrows but don't want to buy them (or don't have the Rupees).

Pond of Happiness (G7/C)

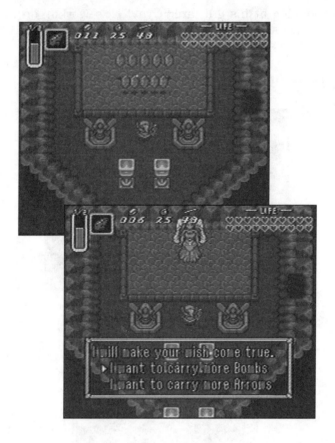

Happy happy, joy joy! By throwing Rupees into the Pond, you increase your Happiness rating. When your Happiness reaches 100 (which occurs after you've thrown in 100 Rupees), a Faerie appears and offers to increase the amount of Bombs or Arrows that you can carry. Come here whenever you have Rupees to burn to increase your Bomb- and Arrow-carrying capacity.

Rupee Room (C8/C)

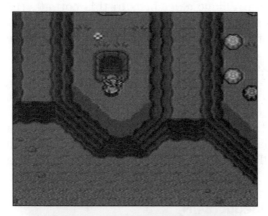

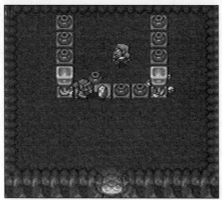

There are two large rocks just southwest of the Middle-Aged Man. Pick up the lower of the two rocks to reveal a hidden set of stairs. Go down the stairs to find ten jars, each of which has five Rupees underneath it. (That's a total of 50 Rupees, but you knew that.) If you leave the Rupee Room and come back, the Rupees regenerate, making this the best location in LTP to boost your Rupee total (although the Shooting Gallery in the Dark World is more fun).

Sahasralah's Cottage (B4/N)

The Kakariko Village elder lives in this cottage. He's about as helpful as a tree stump, unfortunately, although he does give you a bit of information at the very beginning of the game.

Sahasralah's Hideout (G4/N)

The wise and powerful Sahasralah has unwisely set up camp right next to the Eastern Palace. Sahasralah has the Pegasus Shoes, but he won't hand them over until you bring him the first Pendant from the Eastern Palace. Bomb through the north wall to find a hidden room with three Rupee-filled chests.

Thieves' Hideout (B4/N)

The Hideout is right next door to Sahasralah's Cottage. There are several chests in the basement filled with Rupees. There's also a hidden Container Piece. Bomb through the north wall to find it.

Tower of Hera (E1/N)

The Moon Pearl and the third Pendant are located here.

Waterfall of Wishing (H2/NW)

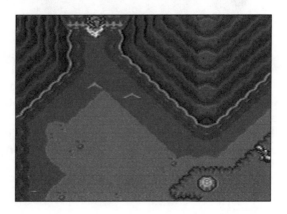

There's a waterfall to the west of the entrance to Zora's Falls. Swim into the falls and you'll enter a hidden cave with a Mysterious Pond. There are three items you can (and should) throw in: the Blue Boomerang, the Fighter's Shield, and empty Magic Bottles. The Faerie turns the Blue Boomerang into the Red Boomerang, turns the Fighter's Shield into the Red Shield, and fills empty Magic Bottles with Green Potion.

Weathercock (B4/C)

Come here with the Flute and give it a toot to free the magic Duck trapped inside the Weathercock and give yourself a spiffy way of getting around the Light World.

DARK WORLD LOCATIONS

Blacksmith's House (C4/SE)

You'll find a Locked Chest in this House once you reunite the Blacksmith Brothers. Hammer down all 22 stakes in the Stake Garden to reveal a hidden cave with a Container Piece inside.

Bomb Shop (E6/N)

The Bomb Shop sells 30 Bombs for 100 Rupees, and (much later in the game) a Super Bomb for 100 Rupees. You don't need to buy the regular Bombs, since you can get them free at the Mysterious Hut, but you will need to buy the Super Bomb in order to reach the Fat Faerie, who you must visit in order to defeat Ganon and complete the adventure.

Dark Castle (H3/S)

The Magic Hammer and the first Crystal are located here.

Fat Faerie (D4/E)

There's a large crack in the Pyramid of Power, near the lowest set of stairs. To blow through this crack, you need the Super Bomb from the Bomb Shop. You'll find a Mysterious Pond in the hidden room; the Fat Faerie lives inside of the Pond.

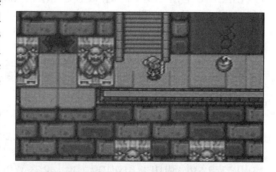

There are two items you can (and should) throw into the Pond: the Tempered Sword and the Bow. The Fat Faerie turns the Tempered Sword into the Golden Sword, and turns your Arrows into Silver Arrows with which to kill Ganon.

Fortune Teller (B3/NE)

The Fortune Tellers give you hints in exchange for Rupees. And since you've got this book, you gotta be nuts to spend any Rupees here.

Game of Chance (A4/E)

For 30 Rupees, you can open two of the 16 treasure chests. You can usually make money at this game. If you're really lucky, you may even find a Container Piece.

Ganon's Tower (E1/C)

The Red Mail and the evil Agahnim are located here.

Gargoyle's Domain (B4/C)

The Titan's Mitt and the fourth Crystal are located here.

Ice Island (G7/C)

The Blue Mail and the fifth Crystal are located here.

Item Shop (C4/NE)

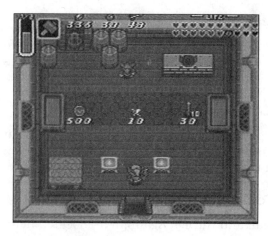

Item Shops are always a waste of time and money, and you should never buy anything from them. You may have to visit this one, however, if your Shield is stolen by a pesky creature called the Pikit. (It's worth noting that you can get a stolen item back from a Pikit if you kill it quickly.)

Misery Maze (A7/NW)

The Cane of Somaria and the sixth Crystal are located here.

Shooting Gallery (B5/S)

For 20 Rupees, you get five arrows to shoot at a moving row of targets. The targets are blocked by a moving row of obstacles that look exactly like the talking hand from the Hamburger Helper commercials. (They do, I swear!)

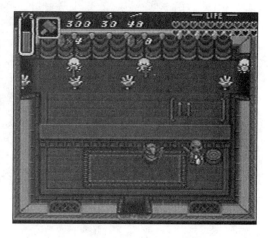

You win 4 Rupees with your first hit, and that amount doubles with each successive hit. If you miss a target, the amount drops back down to 4 Rupees. Here are two scoring examples:

1. Your first shot hits (4 Rupees). Your second shot hits (8 Rupees). Your third shot misses (which drops the amount back down to 4). Your fourth shot hits (4 Rupees). Your fifth shot hits (8 Rupees).

2. All of your shots hit for a total of 124 Rupees (4 + 8 + 16 + 32 + 64).

The key to winning at the Gallery is to wait for a gap in the obstacles. Don't try to fire between the hands. Pick your spots and make your shots.

Skull Palace

The Fire Rod and the third Crystal are located here.

Storyteller (D3/NE)

Pay this Storyteller 20 Rupees and he tells you that normal Bombs can't blow open the cracked wall in the Pyramid of Power. Of course, the last sentence just told you the same thing for free.

Storyteller (G4/C)

This storyteller doesn't charge you any Rupees. Too bad his story isn't of any help. Blow up the north wall behind the Storyteller and walk into the hidden room to find Small Hearts underneath all of the jars. The Hearts regenerate when you leave the building and come back inside, so this is a good place to refill your Heart Containers.

Storyteller (H6/E)

For 20 Rupees, the Storyteller gives you a hint about the circle of stones in the Lake of Ill Omen. (See the Quake Medallion in Chapter 6.)

Storyteller (H6/SW)

"Once upon a time, there was a Storyteller that looked exactly like the talking hand from the Hamburger Helper commercials. (He did, I swear!) He charged 20 Rupees to tell his tale about a former thief that was now posing as the Middle-Aged Man in the Desert of Mystery. Unfortunately for the Storyteller, no one needed to hear his story after reading *this* story. The end."

Swamp Palace (D8/E)

The Hookshot and the second Crystal are located here.

Treasure Field (A6/NE)

For 80 Rupees, you can dig around in the Treasure Field for 30 seconds. You'll find lots of Rupees, but the real prize in the Field is a Container Piece.

Turtle Rock (H1-C)

The Mirror Shield and the seventh Crystal are located here.

Walkthrough

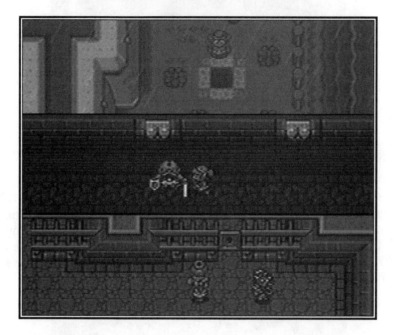

INTRODUCTION

This chapter takes you through LTP from beginning to end. It doesn't mention information that can already be found in earlier chapters, so you'll need to refer to the appropriate chapters for more information on Bosses, Dungeons, Heart Containers, Items, and Locations.

Hyrule Castle

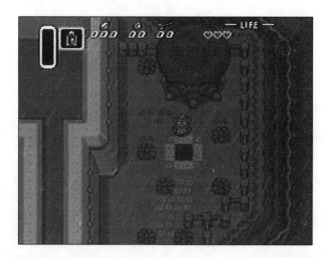

• When your Uncle leaves, jump out of bed and open the chest to collect the Lamp. Go outside and walk north to Hyrule Castle. Cross the bridge, then follow the path leading to the east. Pull up the bush at the end of the path and jump into the hole. Follow the tunnel and you'll find your injured Uncle, who gives you the Fighter's Sword and Fighter's Shield.

• Rescue Zelda and make your way through the dungeons underneath Hyrule Castle. When you arrive in the Sanctuary, talk to the Sage and open the chest for a Heart Container.

Hyrule Heroics

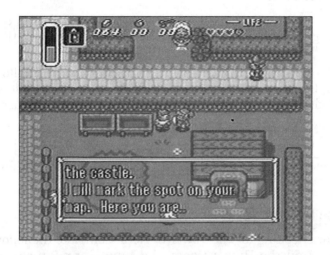

• Go outside and walk to Sahasralah's Cottage. Talk to the village elder to learn some information. Go outside and walk to the small boy at L-B5/NW. Talk to him and he marks the location of Sahasralah on your map.

• Walk to Sahasralah's Palace and talk to him. Bomb through the north wall, walk through, and open the three chests for Bombs and 100 Rupees.

• Before entering the Eastern Palace, complete the following tasks: Buy (or find) some Bombs and blow open the Mysterious Hut. Collect (Heart Container) Pieces 1 through 6. Collect Bottles 1 and 2. Collect the Bug-Catching Net. Find the Magic Mushroom and give it to the Witch.

Eastern Palace

• Collect the Bow and defeat the Armos Knights for the first Pendant.

Hyrule Heroics

• Walk to Sahasralah's Palace and talk to him again to collect the Pegasus Shoes. He'll also remind you to collect the Ice Rod.

• Before entering the Desert Palace, complete the following tasks: Collect Piece 7. Collect the Book of Mudora. Collect the Ice Rod. Collect the Magic Powder from the Witch's House.

Desert Palace

• Collect the Power Glove and defeat the Lanmolas for the second Pendant.

Hyrule Heroics

• Before heading for the Tower of Hera, complete the following tasks: Find the Rupee Room and build your Rupees, then visit the Pond of Happiness to increase your Bomb- and Arrow-carrying capacities. (You don't have to do this right away, and in fact, you can do it a lot faster once you've got

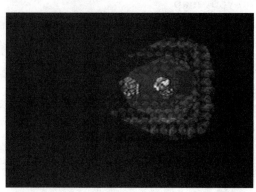

the Flute by flying back and forth between the two locations.) Collect Piece 8. Buy Zora's Flippers. Collect Piece 9. Walk to the Waterfall of Wishing and throw in the Boomerang and Shield. Collect Bottle 3.

• Walk to L-C2/NE and pull up the stone. Enter the cave and you'll meet the Lost Old Man. Walk through the tunnels, following the Old Man's directions. When you emerge from the tunnels atop Death Mountain, the Old Man gives you the Magic Mirror.

• Climb up to Spectacle Rock and collect Piece 10, then make your way to the Tower of Hera. You'll collect Piece 11 on the way to the Tower.

Tower of Hera

• Collect the Moon Pearl and defeat the Moldorm for the third Pendant.

Hyrule Heroics

• Collect the Master Sword and the Ether Medallion. Walk to Hyrule Castle and climb up to Floor 1F. Find the door blocked by a strange beam of light. Swing your Sword at the beam to destroy it and walk through the door.

Hyrule Castle

• Make your way through the Castle and defeat Agahnim. After you defeat him, you'll appear on top of the Pyramid of Power in the Dark World. From this point on, when you go through the front gate of Hyrule Castle, you will warp to the Dark World, appearing in front of the Pyramid of Power.

Hyrule Heroics

• Before entering the Palace of Darkness, collect Pieces 12 and 13 and the Quake Medallion.

Dark Palace

• Collect the Magic Hammer and defeat the Helmasaur King for the first Crystal.

Hyrule Heroics

• Before entering the Watergate Dungeon, collect Pieces 14 through 16, the Bombos Medallion, the Shovel, and the Flute. Go to the Weathercock and play the Flute to free the Duck. Go to the Smithy's Well and use the Magic Powder on the statue.

Swamp Palace

• Collect the Hookshot and defeat Arrghus for the second Crystal.

Hyrule Heroics

• Before entering the Skull Palace, collect the Magic Cape and Pieces 17 through 19.

Skull Palace

• Collect the Fire Rod and defeat Mothula for the third Crystal.

Hyrule Heroics

• There's nothing to do except fill up your Bottles with Magic Potions and enter the Gargoyle's Domain.

Gargoyle's Domain

• Collect the Titan's Mitt and defeat Blind the Thief for the fourth Crystal.

Hyrule Heroics

• Before entering Ice Island, collect Piece 20, the Tempered Sword, Bottle 4, and the Cane of Byrna.

Ice Island

• Collect the Blue Mail and defeat Kholdstare for the fifth Crystal.

Hyrule Heroics

• Before entering the Misery Maze, collect Pieces 21 and 22.

Misery Maze

• Collect the Cane of Somaria and defeat Vitreous for the sixth Crystal.

Hyrule Heroics

• Open the door to Turtle Rock, and collect Piece 23 before going inside.

Turtle Rock

• Collect the Mirror Shield and defeat Trinexx for the seventh Crystal. Collect Piece 24 before you complete the dungeon.

Hyrule Heroics

• Walk west to Ganon's Tower and the seven Crystals open the door.

Ganon's Tower

• Collect the Red Mail and defeat Agahnim a second time. Ganon's spirit flees Agahnim's body and flies to the Pyramid of Power. The Duck flies onto the screen and takes to you the Pyramid.

Hyrule Heroics

• Collect the Golden Sword and Silver Arrows, then climb to the top of the Pyramid of Power and drop into the hole. Defeat Ganon and you've won the game.

CHAPTER
8
Weird, Wild Stuff

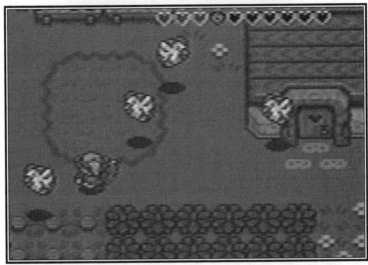

INTRODUCTION

Okay, so the name of this chapter is a fragment of an aging catchphrase from *Saturday Night Live* (Dana Carvey doing Johnny Carson ... you know the one). It's still the perfect way to describe the information in this chapter, and it's my way of paying a humble tribute to Dana, who happens to be my idol. (In fact, I can speak to other people using only Dana's catchphrases, a talent with limited applications at best. But I digress.) Read on and prepare to say "I did not know that ..."

Chicken Attack

If you corner a chicken (in either the Light or Dark World) and attack it repeatedly with your Sword, a flock of chickens eventually attacks you. This is undoubtedly the most bizarre sight in the game.

Flying Fish

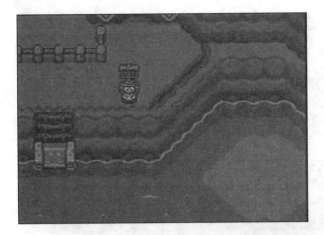

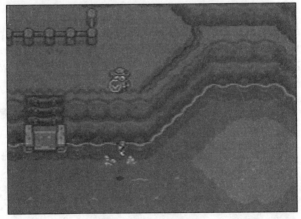

Throw Bombs and other items into bodies of water and watch for fish to make a splash. In the Dark World, fish skeletons jump out of the water instead of fish. Gross.

Great Swamp Fish

When you drain the water in the Great Swamp via the Watergate, and go outside, you'll see two fish flopping around on the ground. There are two things you can do with these fish to make a few Rupees.

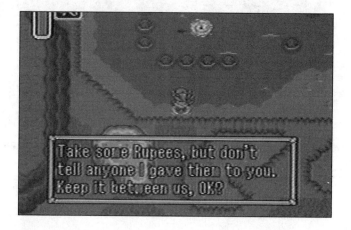

1. Take a fish north to the small lake and throw it in. It gives you a reward of 20 Rupees.

2. Carry a fish up to the Merchant in Kakariko Village (L-B4/W). You can drop the fish to fight enemies along the way. Just make sure the fish stays on the screen or it disappears. The Merchant gives you Rupees and other goodies in exchange for the fish.

Great Swamp Hares

At the beginning of the game, a group of hares lives in the grass of the Great Swamp. When a hare jumps into the air,

chop down the grass underneath and wait for it to hit the ground. Grab the hare and it gives you an item or a few Rupees. (Later on in the game, the hares don't appear any more.)

Lefty Link

In the original Legend of Zelda, Link was a righty, but in LTP, he's a lefty—except when he's facing east. Nintendo of America Inc.'s explanation for this anomaly is that Link keeps his shield pointed at Death Mountain out of superstitious

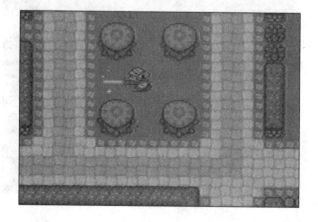

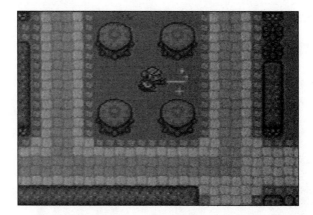

fear. The real reason for Link's ambidextrous sword-swinging: to save on memory, the programmers use the same graphics when Link is facing east or west, flipping them in the appropriate direction.

Running Man

There's a man dressed in red on the road just north of the small boy in Kakariko Village (L-B5/NW). If you have the Pegasus Shoes, you can catch the man as he starts to run away from you. When you nab him, he'll tell you about Dashing into trees to knock out items.

Sweeping Lady

Look for the woman at L-B5/NW, sweeping her front porch. Sprinkle Magic Powder on her and she turns into a Faerie. Go into her house and Bomb through the east wall to find ten Arrows in a hidden chest. When you leave the house, the Sweeping Lady reappears, and you can turn her into a Faerie again (and again and again).

Talking Trees

Some of the trees in the Dark World are mucho talkative. If you see a tree with "eyes" that follow you around, bump into the tree and press the A button to talk to it. Talking trees spit out Bombs before they start jabbering, so watch yourself.

Link's Awakening

THE LIBRARY

There are eight books in the Mabe Village Library, each containing information that is useful in your adventure. If you don't have the time to visit the library in person, you can read their contents here and now!

"Selecting the Item That's Right for You"

You can select your favorite item for the A and B buttons on the sub-screen. Using different items, you can fight without a sword! Try many different things to find what's right for you!

"Auto Map and Memo Guide Book"

You can see an island map by pressing the Select button. The dark parts of the map are places you haven't yet visited. Move the cursor and press the A button to get more information about an area, or to replay the message you got there.

"Secrets of the Whirling Blade"

The Whirling Blade technique has been handed down from generation to generation by the family of the hero. To use it, hold down the sword button and build up your power. When you have enough, you can release the button!

"How to Handle your Shield Like a Pro"

If you hold the button down, you can defend yourself from enemy attacks. You can flip some enemies, too... Besides the standard shield, there is also a mirrored variety which can defend against beams!

"Fun with Bombs"

After you put a bomb down, you can pick it up by pressing the button again. You can then throw it by pushing the button one more time.

"The Properties of Warp Holes"

There are some warp holes on Koholint Island. You can warp to and fro using these holes. If you jump into the warp hole at which you arrived, you go to the next one in the sequence. You can only warp to a hole you have seen with your own eyes.

"Dark Secrets and Mysteries of Koholint"

Round and round, the passageways of the Egg...
    Hmmmmmm, this book reeks of secrets...
    Note: The directions you must take inside the Egg are random—they change for each new game.

"Atlas of Koholint Island"

You can move the cursor and look up the name of a place. Here they all are, for reference.

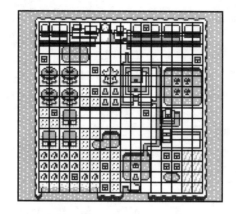

Animal Village	M13-N13, M14-N14
Cemetery	G7-H7, G8-H8
Crazy Tracy's Health Spa	F5
Dream Shrine	D9
East of the Bay	M15-N15, M16-N16
Face Shrine	N9, M10-N10, M11-P11, M12-P12
Fishing Pond	B9
Goponga Swamp	A3-D3, C4-E4
Hen House	K1
House by the Bay	G16
Kanalet Castle	I5-K5, I6-L6, I7-L7, I8-L8
Koholint Prairie	E5, E6-F6, E7, E8-F8
Level 1—Tail Cave	D14
Level 2—Bottle Grotto	E3
Level 3—Key Cavern	F12
Level 4—Angler's Tunnel	L3
Level 5—Catfish's Maw	J14
Level 6—Face Shrine	M9
Level 7—Eagle's Tower	O1
Level 8—Turtle Rock	A2
Mabe Village	C10, A11-D11
Madam MeowMeow's House—Beware of Dog!	B11

Marin and Tarin's House	C11
Martha's Bay	I13-L13, I14-K14, G15-L15, H16-L16
Mt. Tamaranch	G1, G2-H2
Mysterious Woods	A5-D5, A6-D6, A7-D7, A8-D8, A9, A10-B10
Old Man Ulrira's House	B12
Pothole Field	G13-H13, H14
Quadruplet's House	C9
Raft Shop	P4
Rapids Ride	M5-P5, M6-P6, M7-P7, M8-P8, O9-P9, O10-P10
Richard's Villa	G14
Sale's House O' Bananas	D15
Seashell Mansion	K9
Signpost Maze	E13-F13, E14-F14
South of the Village	A13-D13, A14-C14
Tabahl Wasteland	G5-H5, G6-H6
Tal Tal Heights	F3-P3, F4-P4
Tal Tal Mountain Range	A1-P1, C2-P2
Telephone Booth	B2, B4, L5, I9, E11, C12, L14, I15
Toronbo Shores	A15-F15, A16-F16
Town Tool Shop	D10
Trendy Game	D12
Ukuku Prairie	E9-L9, E10-L10, E11-L11, E12-L12
Village Library	A12
Weird Mr. Write	A4
Wind Fish's Egg	F1
Witch's Hut	F7
Yarna Desert	O13-P13, O14-P14, O15-P15, O16-P16

MAJOR ITEMS

Sword: At the beginning of the adventure, a sword washes up on Toronbo Shores—it is yours.

Shield: You must activate the shield and press the button to use it against enemy attack.

Magic Power: The Magic Powder is used for sprinkling on special objects. It also lights the torches in dungeons.

Roc's Feather: You can't fly away with this, but it does make Link jump a short distance. With the Pegasus Boots found later, it can be used to jump up to three gaps in the ground.

Pegasus Boots: These mythical boots can be used to make Link dash around, bashing into objects.

Power Bracelet: When this bracelet is active, Link can lift large rocks and plants and throw them at his enemies.

Hookshot: This item hooks onto objects in the distance and pulls Link toward them. It can also attack enemies, while keeping Link out of danger.

Magic Rod: Link can shoot fire using this special weapon. It's useful for melting ice and lighting torches, too.

Bombs: Bombs can be found hidden around, or can be bought from the store. They blow holes in cracked walls!

Bow: If you have arrows to go with it, the bow is a useful long-range weapon. It can also trigger switches.

 Shovel: You can dig up the dirt using this item. Many hearts and Rupees are hidden, along with special items.

 Ocarina: Once you have picked up this musical instrument, you can learn three tunes to play that have special effects.

 Boomerang: As it hits an enemy as you throw it and on its return, this is a powerful weapon.

 Flippers: You can swim around the lakes and rivers, and even dive when you wear these.

 Map: Inside a level, you get around much easier if you find the map. It highlights all the rooms.

 Compass: Picking this up shows you the locations of all the treasure and nightmare creatures in a level.

 Stone Slab: Dotted around each level you find stones with writing on. You can only read the stones if you fill in the blanks.

Other Items

Sleepy Mushroom: This is a very rare fungus. It must be dug up and given to the witch for magic powder.

Yoshi Doll: These cool dolls can be won in the Trendy Game. It must be given to a house with children.

Secret Shells: You find these all over the island. When you have collected 20, you can visit the Seashell Mansion and buy the level two sword.

Secret Medicine: If you carry this in your backpack, all your energy is restored when you die.

Gold Leaf: Return this to its rightful owner for a special reward.

Level Keys: Each level needs the right key to open the main door. You must search for these all over the island.

Small Keys: You earn these by killing creatures, then opening the treasure chests that appear.

Nightmare Keys: These special keys are needed to open the door to the boss in each level.

Rupees: These are collected from the start. Pick up or win as many as possible to spend in stores.

Hearts: Each heart you pick up fills one container. They are found when enemies are killed, or by cutting the grass.

Heart Pieces and Containers: Four pieces are needed to make one container, or you can win one by defeating a big boss.

Winged Items: If an item is hovering with wings, you must use the Roc's Feather to reach it.

Faeries: These kind creatures restore some of your energy. They usually appear after defeating sub-bosses.

Acorns of Defense: If you pick these up, your defensive powers are temporarily increased.

Piece of Power: If an enemy drops one of these triangular items, grab it. It increases your sword's power for a short time.

Instruments of the Sirens: Completing a level earns you one of the Nightmare's Instruments. You need all eight to wake the Wind Fish and complete the game.

TRADING ITEMS

As you play through the adventure, you have to trade with characters to receive certain items. Here is a list of what must be traded for what.

Item wanted	Item needed	Obtained from	Located at
Yoshi Doll	Rupees	Trendy Man	Trendy Game
Ribbon	Yoshi Doll	Quadruplet's Mom	Quadruplet's House
Dog Food	Ribbon	Little BowWow	BowWow's Doghouse

Item wanted	Item needed	Obtained from	Located at
Bananas	Dog Food	Sale	Sale's House O' Bananas
Stick	Bananas	Monkey	Kanalet Castle Bridge
Honeycomb	Stick	Tarin	Ukuku Prairie
Pineapple	Honeycomb	Chef Bear	Animal Village
Hibiscus	Pineapple	Quadruplet's Dad	Tal Tal Heights
Letter	Hibiscus	Miss Goat	Animal Village
Broom	Letter	Mr. Write	Mr. Write's House
Fish Hook	Broom	Grandma Ulrira	Animal Village
Necklace	Fish Hook	Fisherman	Under Bridge
Scale	Necklace	Mermaid	Martha's Bay
Magnifying Glass	Scale	Mermaid Statue	Martha's Bay

SOLUTION

This walkthrough for *The Legend of Zelda: Link's Awakening* shows you the most direct route through the game. In an adventure like this, there are always a multitude of sub-plots and extra sequences to be found and played, but they are not vital. Think of the text as pointing you the right direction, but feel free to explore on your own between locations. This way you get the most out of this wonderful game.

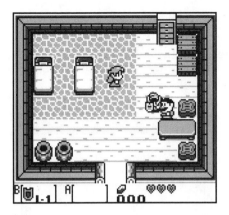

Where am I?

When Link wakes in Tarin and Marin's house, talk to Tarin to get your shield back. With that you can venture out into the outside world and start your adventure.

Head south, moving through Mabe Village to Toronbo Shores. Talk to all the characters you meet along the way for snippets of information that will come in useful later. When you reach the shores, move right to find your sword stuck in the sand. You know it's yours because it has your name on it!

Now head north, back to Mabe Village and on to the Mysterious Woods. Locate the signpost that warns about cracks and enter the wooden tree stump nearby. On the other side you find the Sleepy Mushroom. Now visit the witch in her hut and talk to her. She notices the mushroom and asks if she can use it in her recipe—she gives you 20 Magic Power sprinkles! Another good source of Magic Powder is the Trendy Game back in Mabe Village.

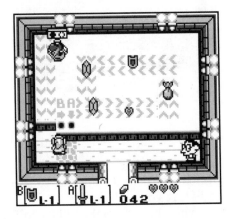

You find a raccoon hiding out in the Mysterious Woods. Sprinkle him with Magic Powder—he turns into Tarin and explains he had a bad dream. Move north from the raccoon screen and get the Tail Key from the treasure chest.

Head back to Mabe and play the Trendy Game to win yourself the Yoshi Doll. Now go to the Quadruplet's House and trade the doll with the Mom for a Ribbon. Visit the smaller dog house outside Madam MeowMeow's House and give the Ribbon to the small BowWow inside. You receives a can of Dog Food. Head north from Mabe to the Fishing Pond and pay the man. Fish until you catch a lurker (runts are no good). That done, make your way to Sale's House O' Bananas.

Sale collects cans of food and wants to trade Dog Food for Bananas—do it! Make sure you have some bombs in your inventory (if you don't, go to the store and buy some; you will have to buy the shovel first, though). Now you can head south to the Tail Cave.

Level 1: Tail Cave

Use the key you collected earlier in the central statue to open the door. Inside the cave you find the Roc's Feather and an array of new enemies.

Card creatures are particularly tricky to kill. When you hit them, they stop on the suit they were showing at the time. Stop all three on the same suit to make them disappear and a treasure chest appear.

Always look out for patterns in the blocks and floor in the caves and dungeons. Sometimes arrows are formed that show you where to bomb, or pushing blocks into a pattern can trigger a chest to appear.

The beetles in Tail Cave must be flipped over with the shield before you can stab and kill them.

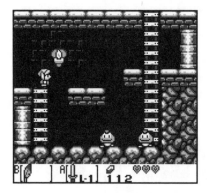 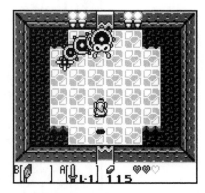

Boss 1: Moldorm

Your first boss encounter is a giant worm that wiggles its way around the screen, bouncing off the walls. Make sure you keep your back to the wall at all times, and run left and right to avoid him running into you—watching out for the pit. Moldorm's only weak spot is his tail. Strike him here with the sword three times and you will conquer him.

The reward is a heart container and the first Nightmare Instrument: the Full Moon Cello.

Return to Mabe Village and you discover that the Moblins have attacked and BowWow has been dognapped. Head north through the Mysterious Woods, then on to the Tal Tal Heights. You find a cave to enter—inside you can rescue BowWow by defeating the boss guard.

The trick here is to wait until the guard hits his head against the wall. He's dizzy for a short period, which is when you should strike with the sword. Two hits is enough.

Return BowWow to Madam MeowMeow and she thanks you, then asks if you can take him for a walk! Take BowWow north to the Goponga Swamp, where he eats flowers, allowing Link to get through. Find the entrance to the Bottle Grotto and BowWow stays outside.

Level 2: Bottle Grotto

The Power Bracelet is found on this level, in a room with two ghosts. Simply use the magic powder on the torches to light up the room and scare the ghosts away. To defeat Hinox the cyclops, avoid his bombs then dash-attack with your sword before running out of his range.

You may find a platform that won't lower on one of the side-scrolling sections. Simply pick up the pot and carry it with you to weigh the platform down.

To find the boss area, pay attention to the stone slab and kill the creatures in the southern room in the correct order. First kill the bat, then Stalfos the rabbit, and finally the robed skeleton.

Boss 2: The Genie

When the Genie throws fireballs, get into the bottom-right corner of the screen and run to the left as the fireballs fly. When he's released three, he returns to his bottle. Attack the bottle with the sword, then pick it up with the Power Bracelet and throw it at the wall to smash it. Repeat this three times to enter the final phase.

The Genie sends out spinning versions of himself. Have the sword and feather ready and stay at the bottom of the screen. When he becomes one, charge at him and swipe with the sword. Repeat this a couple of times and you win a heart and Conch Horn.

Head back to Mabe Village and return BowWow to his house. Locate Richard's Villa on the map and head there. Chat with Richard and he asks you to return the five Golden Leaves from Kanalet Castle. Best foot forward, get to the castle, heading north-east from Richard's Villa. If you get lost, follow the signposts.

Around the side of the castle you find Kiki the monkey. Give him the bananas when he asks and he calls other monkeys, who create a bridge for you to cross. Pick up the stick on the bridge and use it to enter the castle by bashing a bush. Now you need to find the five leaves.

Leaf one is acquired by killing the mad bomber—use a pot to break open his door. The raven in the gardens hides the sec-ond—first throw a stone to disturb him, then swing with your sword. One of the first guards inside the castle has the third, then bombing and killing the hidden guard out of the wall (look for his eyes) gives a fourth. Finally, the fifth leaf is earned by killing the mole that's throwing bombs in the eastern garden.

Return to Richard's Villa and chat with him, then move on to the field outside the house and use the shovel to dig under the owl statue. You find the Slime Key. Head east of the bush garden, around the trees and then west, jumping over the water.

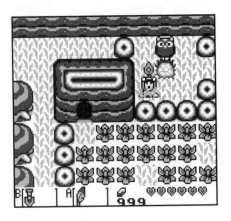

Level 3: Key Cavern

Use the Slime Key to open up the Key Cavern. Inside you find the Pegasus Boots hidden in a treasure chest.

In one room you will find two black snakes slithering about. The only way to kill these is to drop three bombs in front of them. They gobble them up, then explode! You need to practice dash-jumping to cross one large hole in this cavern too—take a run up then use the feather at the last minute to clear the gap. Always remember to kill all enemies in each room to earn small keys.

Boss 3: Slime Eyes

You can't see this boss at first, but use the boots to dash into the wall and a pair of sinister eyes fall from the ceiling. Dash-attack where they are joined together to split them into two roaming eyes, making them far easier to pick off with your sword. Defeat this beast and you earn the Lily Bell.

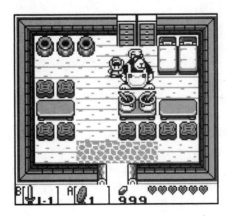

Now that you have the Pegasus Boots, visit the Dream Shrine in Mabe Village. You find the Ocarina. Take this instrument to

Marin at the weathercock and she sings "The Ballad of the Wind Fish" for you to learn and play.

Find Ukuku Prairie and send Link off there. When you find Tarin wandering around, give him the stick and you will get the Honeycomb.

You must now visit the Animal Village at the southern end of the island. This is an enchanted village where animals talk. Visit the house with the Bear Cook and give him the Honeycomb—he gives you the Pineapple. The bear also tells you that Marin's special song will wake up the Walrus that sleeps nearby.

Return to Mabe to find Marin, but she will have moved from the weathercock. If you ask the small boy in the village, he tells you that she likes to visit Toronbo Shores sometimes. And sure enough, you find her on the far eastern shore. After chatting with her for a while, return to the Animal Village (via a warp hole, if you wish) with Marin in tow. Take her to the Walrus and she sings her song, making him disappear. Now you can access Yarna Desert.

There's a sub-boss to defeat in the desert, a sandworm named Lanmola. Kill him by hitting him on the head—no other part of his body is vulnerable. When you have defeated him, find the Angler Key and quckly pick it up, or it will be sucked down by the sand. If it does, you will find it in the cave below, along with a piece of heart.

Go back north to the Tamaranch Mountains. You can use the Angler Key on the keyhole found on the river path—it makes the cave entrance appear from behind a waterfall. Travel on up into the mountains and you find Papahl, who told you he would be there. He's exhausted, so give him the pineapple to revitalize him and in return you receive the Hibiscus flower.

To enter the Angler's Tunnel, walk to the top of the mountain and take a leap of faith to land in front of the entrance.

Level 4: Angler's Tunnel

The Flippers are found inside the cave, in the northwestern room. To get past the room with tiles on the ground, watch the sequence they flash in then repeat it without making a mistake. Get it right to receive the Nightmare Key.

You need to use the Power Bracelet to pull a lever in one room, making two blocks pull apart. Be quick and you'll make it through the door. Once the Flippers have been collected, you can swim around and dive in the deep water. This allows you to access places you couldn't before.

Boss 4: Angler Fish

This giant fish has one weak spot to look out for—a glowing feeler on his back. There are no real tactics to defeat this creature; simply equip your sword and go crazy with it whenever the fish comes near. You will soon land him, and earn the Surf Harp from the next room.

Go west from the exit of the Angler's Tunnel and you find another cave. Inside is Manbo, who teaches you a second song to play on your Ocarina. Each time you play this song, you're transported to Manbo's Pond, near Crazy Tracy's house—you can visit her to collect a heart-restoring potion. Playing the tune inside a cave takes you to its entrance instead, which is very useful sometimes.

Wander around for a short time and a ghost appears. It asks you to take it to the small hut near the bay, so do as it says. After reminiscing for a while, it asks to be taken to its grave. Head toward the cemetery, but instead of going into the main tombstone area, go to the single tombstone on the other side of the Witch's Hut.

Level 5: Catfish's Maw

Make sure you have a good stock of Rupees (if you need more, you can win plenty on the Trendy Game) and head down to Catfish's Maw. To get inside, dive down underneath the rocks to the west.

Inside this cave you find the Hookshot after defeating Master Stalfos, the skeleton in four separate rooms. You can tell which order to play the rooms in by the number of blocks in the corners. To kill him, slash at him with your sword, then when he's dazed, place a bomb on top of him!

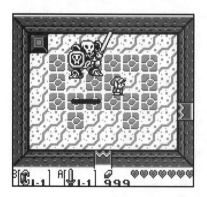

Boss 5: Slime Eel

Four holes surround this arena, and the Eel's head pops out from all of them, while his tail slashes around in the center. Stay in the middle of the arena and jump the tail, then use the Hookshot to pull the heads from their holes.

If you find a head with a heart attached to it, it's the real Eel—the others are fakes. Hit the heart a few times and he gives it up, earning you the Wind Marimba.

Back to the Animal Village now, give the Hibiscus to Ms. Goat in her house. She gives you a letter that she would like taken to Mr. Write. Look at the letter and it's a picture of a girl called Christine, who looks strangely like Zelda! Deliver the letter to Mr. Write's house in the northwest and you get a Broom in return.

If you explored the Animal Village properly you will know that Ulrira's wife needs a new broom, so go there and give it to her. You get the Fishing Hook as a reward. Take it to Martha's Bay and find the timber bridge you can dive underneath, where you discover a fisherman. Give him the hook and he says he'll give you his next catch in return. It turns out to be the Mermaid's necklace.

Now find the Mermaid swimming around in the bay. Return the necklace and she lets you have a Scale from her tail. You can use this scale on the mermaid statue nearby to discover the Magnifying Glass.

If you have collected more than 300 Rupees (you can always try out the cheat on the store to get more), visit the Signpost Maze in the south. Follow the instructions on the posts, moving to the next one in the direction shown to follow the trail. Get it wrong and you have to start over, but get it right and you arrive at Mamu the frog. Pay him the cash and he lets you learn his song for your Ocarina.

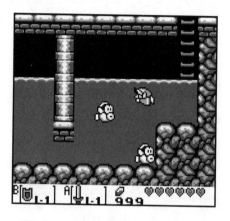

For a bit of fun, and to collect some power-ups, you can take a ride on the Rapids about now. Use the Hookshot to access the Raft Shop, then use the feather to jump up and collect the items as you pass underneath.

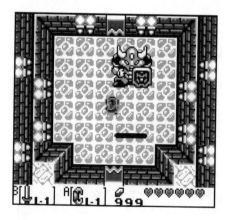

Level 6: Face Shrine

Time to visit the Face Shrine. There are in fact two shrines to visit—enter the southern one first to find the Face Key. You need to defeat the Armos Knight before you can take the key away, but he's quite easy to kill. You need to shoot him with around 12 arrows. When he's dead, pick up the key, then go north into the next room and take a look at the painting of the Wind Fish.

Now you can use the Face Key to enter the second shrine. Go left when inside to acquire the second level Power Bracelet. With this in your inventory, Link can pick up the large elephant-shaped blocks and smash them into doors.

There's a tricky sub-boss in here, a little guy who throws a cue ball at you. Simply pick it up and throw it back at him a few times.

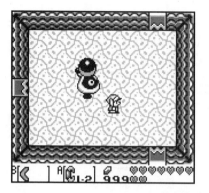

Boss 6: Facade

You need to get your shield equipped and ready for this boss, as floor tiles will come flying toward Link's face. When they have died down, simply place bombs on the Facade and he explodes after a while. You get the Coral Triangle.

To help you through some tricky spots in the next part of the adventure, you need to find the Rooster. Unfortunately, he's dead. But don't fret, you can bring him back to life. Go to the weather-cock in Mabe and push it aside (with the new Power Bracelet, you now have the strength). Go down the steps and find the Rooster, then play the third song you have collected on your Ocarina. This brings him back to life.

Before you do anything else now, head for Toronbo Shores once again. Enter the cave down here and you discover a guy who offers to trade whatever you have in your B button for a Boomerang. This weapon is worth getting, so choose something you won't need anymore (like the Shovel) and get the weapon. With this you can then clear a bush field south of Martha's Bay, then land with the Rooster and find a Genie who gives you more bombs or arrows.

With the Rooster up and running, head to the northeast and into the mountains again. You need to locate the Hen House, then the cave nearby. In here you find the Bird Key. With the key, go east to the Eagle's Tower.

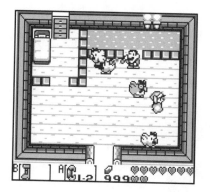 

Level 7: Eagle's Tower

Throw the rocks out of the way, then put the key into the lock to start the tower rotating and reveal the entrance. Inside you earn the level two Mirror Shield. This cave is laid out in a different way to the others—it's on four levels. If you fall through a gap in the ground on a higher level, you fall through to the lower one. This can make things quite disorientating.

The main objective in this level is to find the black ball on floor one, then use it to demolish the four pillars. You need to use bombs to blow holes in cracked walls. Small keys can be found in the chests on the ledges of floor one. To reach the ledges you need to drop through from above.

The Grim Creeper sub-boss is quite a slippery customer. He commands six bats to attack you at once. You must destroy all of them before they fly off the screen, or they reform and attack again.

Boss 7: Evil Eagle

Link climbs to the top of the mountain to tackle the eagle. This giant bird has a variety of attacks, ranging from simple sweeps to flying feathers and a devastating wing flap that can blow Link right off his perch!

When the wings are flapping, have the Pegasus Boots equipped and run in the opposite direction. Swipe your sword at the bird whenever he gets too close. When he fires feathers at you, use the shield to deflect them. Eventually you'll win, and Link can climb back down and enter the room to find the Organ of Evening Calm.

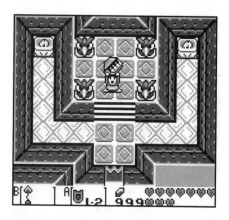

In the far west of the mountains is another Genie, who grants you more arrows or bombs if you need them. When you arrive outside Turtle Rock, the guardian of the rock is sleeping. Play the third song ("The Song of Soul") on your Ocarina to wake him up. Now kill him and you can access the cave.

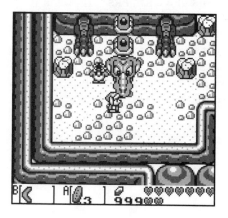

Level 8: Turtle Rock

Inside Turtle Rock you need to learn how to use the movable platforms effectively. Remember, when manipulating a moving platform, don't take your fingers off the D-pad, or it will stop. Filling up all the gaps with the platform triggers hidden small keys to fall from the ceiling or a treasure chest to appear.

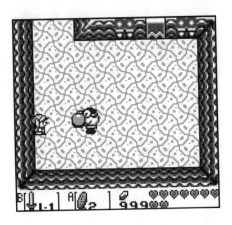

Other tricky spots include shooting an arrow into the eye of a statue for a key, and Blaino the boxing kangaroo. You must hit this guy from the sides or back; he's in invulnerable from the front. Use the feather to jump around him while he is punching, then go in for the attack. He's a tough cookie to crack, as one punch from his glove knocks Link back to the beginning of Turtle Rock!

When you defeat Blaino, go into the room north of his lair and get the Rod of Fire. This allows you to melt ice blocks in the underground passageways, giving access to the final section of the level. Always remember to melt the ice blocks in such a way as to leave yourself a stairway of ice to climb up.

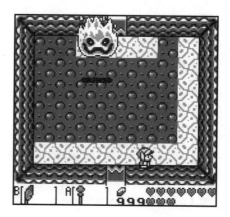

Boss 8: Hot Head

This guy lives and breathes fire—literally. He's a dancing flame that hops around the room, launching fireballs. Fight fire with fire, using the freshly acquired Rod of Fire. Let out as many shots as you possibly can—if enough hit him, he gives up and you receive the Thunder Drum.

With all eight Nightmare Instruments under your belt, it's time to go visit the giant Egg that sits on top of the mountain in the north of the island. Climb up to the top and play "The Ballad of the Wind Fish." The instruments circle around the egg and it will crack, allowing Link to access its yolky interior.

Unfortunately, the Egg is one giant maze of identical rooms, so you won't get anywhere if you go right on in. First travel all the way back to Mabe Village and go to the Library. Use the Magnifying Glass collected earlier to read the third book along on the bottom row—"Dark Secrets and Mysteries of Koholint." This book gives you a set of directions to follow. They differ each time you play the game, so you always need to visit the Library before entering the Egg.

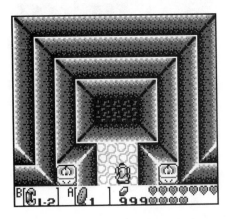

With these directions safely written down, make sure you have good stocks of all weapons, then go back to the Egg and on inside.

It's dark inside the Egg, but head north and fall down. Now use those directions to find yourself in front of another pit. Fall into this one and prepare to take on the Nightmares, the final batta%s of Link's Awakening.

The Nightmares

Nightmare 1: The Giant Gel

The first Nightmare boss is a blob of gel that oozes around the arena. It's simple to dispose of. Just sprinkle Magic Powder on him three times to send him on his way.

Nightmare 2: Agahnim's Shadow

Agahnim appeared in the Super NES *A Link to the Past* and likes to charge up his magic attack and blast it out. All you need to do is stand opposite him when he releases his magic, then send it back at him with the sword. Return a few blasts and he gives up.

Nightmare 3: Moldorm

You have already beaten Moldorm once, so he shouldn't be too tricky. Simply attack his tail again, but have the shield at the ready in case he decides to charge at you. Three slashes should be enough.

Nightmare 4: Ganon's Shadow

This guy was the main boss in previous Zelda games, so if you have played any of those, you'll know what to do: You need to equip the Pegasus Boots and the Sword and charge at him relentlessly. Attack furiously and you'll soon send him running.

Nightmare 5: Lanmola

You will never fight an easier boss than Lanmola. All you need to do is equip the Hookshot and send one in his general direction. If it hits home, you have done it!

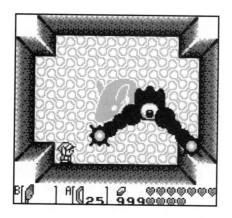

Nightmare 6: Dethl

Finally, the ultimate boss of The Legend of Zelda: Link's Awakening. Dethl has two long arms that swing around the arena, and a giant eye that opens from time to time. You need to equip both the feather and arrows to beat him.

Stay at the bottom of the arena and use the feather to jump his arms, if they swing in your direction. Trace his movements left and right, and each time he opens his eye, send an arrow into it. You may need up to 20 arrows to kill him.

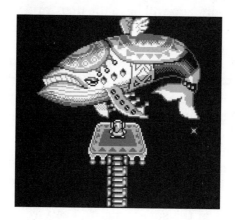

With all that done, the Wind Fish awakens and you're treated to the end sequence. What a rewarding game to play!

GAME SECRETS

The Legend of Zelda: Link's Awakening is packed with secrets and bugs that help you out of sticky situations.

- If you enter "ZELDA" as your name at the start, all the background music is different.

- You may think that whacking chickens is fun, but if you stick at it long enough, a whole flock rushes on and attacks you!

- If you don't have enough Rupees to buy an item you need, you can steal it instead! All you have to do is pick the item up and run around the shopkeeper to make him face away from the door. When he's facing in the other direction, quickly run out and the item's yours! The game tells you that you have stolen it and asks if you're proud of yourself. The side effects of this are that from then on, your name is THIEF instead of whatever you entered, and on returning to the shop, the shopkeeper will kill you!

- You can spend less on an item without being branded a thief by pressing A, B, Select, and Start when the shopkeeper starts to take your money. Save and Quit on the menu screen and start again. You will have the item, and your money will be intact.

- You can create a powerful weapon by selecting both the bombs and arrows at the same time. Press A and B together to send a burning explosive arrow across the screen!

- When you are with Marin, she nags at you if you break pots or attack chickens, but take her to the Trendy Game for a great laugh. She takes the controls and picks up the Trendy Man instead!

- When you have the Rooster tagging along, and have the Power Bracelet and Boomerang in your inventory, you can create a mean killing machine! Simply grab the Rooster's legs and fire a boomerang at the same time. You can fly around, with the Boomerang circling you, smashing enemies to kingdom come!

- If you want to cheat your way through, look for exits in a room opposite entrances. If you walk off the last room then hit Select instantly, occasionally you're put back into the game